INMATE #02071987

KIERRA WALKER

CONTENTS

CHAPTER 1

As an adult, I've found myself pondering over ordeals that seemed mountainous and undefeatable in my younger years. Like the time I stopped speaking to my sister because she broke something of mine that had sentimental value, or the instance when I called myself running away. After all, my father and I disagreed. I can only laugh, as the knowledge I have now would have been useful then. Thinking back, I could have saved the dramatics for a time when I'd need them most. Unfortunately, life doesn't work that way; there's always a lesson to be had.

My mother's most prized line of advice was consistent. During hardships, she'd be the first to cease, gather hands, and pray. Despite life's circumstances, she always had powerful, encouraging words to share with us. Her favorite thing to say was,

"The Lord shall put no more on you than you can bear."

No matter if it was a prayer before dinner or travel, she'd make that statement. Of all the life values she worked tirelessly as a single mother to ingrain in my sister and me throughout childhood, this value was most prominent for me. Little did I know, I'd be chomping at the bit, exerting every fiber of my being, to preserve my sanity using that phrase alone.

For the last hour, I've been sitting in my vehicle, staring into the distance, trying to decide whether I want to get out or not. I drive and park in this exact spot from time to time, but lately, my coming here has been less frequent. I take a moment to gather my thoughts, inhaling and exhaling deeply. Reluctant, and rather anxious, I resolve to open the door of my SUV and step out. I reposition my clothing and grab my belongings from the center console, locking my eyes on my destination. Putting one foot in front of the other, I tread lightly in my kitten heels over the uneven gravel until I reach solid ground.

From my small bag, I pull out a medium-sized blanket, spreading it over the ground right before my feet. I remove my shoes and crouch down until I'm on my bottom.

"Hey, honey, it's me..." I say aloud, raking random leaves from the tombstone.

Samuel E. Bennett
Sunrise: January 21, 1969
Sunset: June 1, 2014
Beloved Husband and Father

"Sam, it's been five years and I miss you as if you just parted from this earth yesterday," I express softly to myself at the head of my husband's grave.

Samuel E. Bennett, or Sammie as I would call him, was my husband of 27 years. Through mutual friends, we became acquainted during halftime at one of his basketball games. There was an instant attraction. We exchanged numbers and started courting, with our parents' permission of course. Our parents didn't object; we could simply be two young people in love. Following high school, we made an abrupt decision to wed. We opted out of the traditional manners of marriage and wed, with our best friends as witnesses, at a small, dank, outdated courthouse in the downtown area of our hometown. I can't necessarily say that our parents were thrilled, but they accepted the decision. Many couples experience negativity in their marriages, whether it's due to finances, their feelings, etc., but it wasn't that way for Sammie and me I. Sure we had our arguments, but our love for one another was pure, stimulating, just one-of-a-kind.

Two nights before his passing, Sammie complained of chest pain. Unaware of what the cause could be, I rushed him to the emergency room. On arrival, we were rushed to a private room and he was examined. They performed a variety of tests, only to conclude that Sammie was experiencing heartburn. They provided us with instructions for over-the-counter medication and handed over discharge papers. The next night I was awakened by Sammie's fumbling, he was gasping, fighting for his life. I called 911 and made a last-ditch effort to pull him from bed and rush him to the hospital myself, but he didn't want that. He clutched me by the wrist, shuddering, shaking his head no. When I asked why he clutched me harder. He couldn't say it, but I firmly believe he knew it was his time. I leaned in, whispering, "I love you," as tears streamed from his eyes, down over his cheeks, and onto his chest. My husband, my Sammie, passed away right there in my arms; the ambulance arrived shortly after.

I take the next ten minutes to hold a one-sided conversation with my deceased husband, realizing I needed to move on. As I did before, I take the blanket and spread it before my feet. This time, in front of a different gravesite. As I stoop down, I see that the flat gravestone before me is covered in soil and foliage. Faintly disheartened by the condition of the gravestone, I use my left hand to uncover it, revealing someone that I recall all too well.

In Loving Memory Of
Samara Brielle Bennett
Sunrise: February 7, 1987
Sunset: July 31, 2015
Your Light Will Shine Forever

My sweet Samara Brielle, my one and only daughter, my firstborn.

"A mother isn't supposed to outlive her child..." I jolt, fighting back the same tears I'd previously shed for my husband.

Only, these tears were different. As if it weren't enough to lose my husband, I lost my child in just over a year. I had absolutely no time to mourn the loss of my husband before being burdened with the untimely demise of my daughter.

"Each time I come and go, it becomes increasingly difficult to manage, to continue coming back. Mama's so sorry she's waited weeks to return," I mumble, wiping away the remaining soil from Samara's headstone.

As always, I'm emotionally overcome by memories from Samara's childhood, causing tears to flow like a raging river.

"It's not right, existing here on this earth without you. I've been robbed of my opportunity to witness you blossom into the woman you had only dreamt of becoming. After four years I imagined coping, dealing with your premature death would be easier; boy I was wrong. Daily I find myself curing God, asking him why he took you and not me! It's not fair! I'd give my life in a heartbeat to hear your voice one last time, to stop you from traveling to your destination that day, to keep you home and sheltered from this cruel world," frustration exudes me with each word.

I take a moment to recompose, wiping away the last bit of my tears, careful not to smudge my makeup.

"I can't stay long but I brought you something..." I clear my throat, reaching in my bag. Golden colored Calla Lilies; a dozen of them. They were her favorite. I lay them before Samara's headstone and begin to gather the items I'd brought along with me.

As I stand, the wind whistles, rapidly circling my body. My body is overcome by an instant chill, creating goosebumps from head to toe. I open my arms as if I'm receiving a hug, imagining the wind being Sammie and Samara embracing me. I succumb, and as quickly as it started it ends. They're gone.

———

Walking into my foyer, I drop my purse and keys on the console table, kick my shoes off, heading for my favorite spot; the loveseat. I plop down, throwing my head back on the couch. I need a moment to close my eyes, I need to meditate and practice my breathing techniques. As I get in the groove, I hear the door leading from the kitchen to the garage open and close.

"Hey, you're home early. How was your day?"

"Hey, baby, it was fine. How was yours?"

"I have no complaints. The coach had us lift weights today,

so my body is sore and I'm equally as tired. What's for dinner?" Sean probes, sitting beside me.

"I don't know, what would you like?" I yawn, tapping him on the thigh.

"I was hoping we could have your famous meatloaf..."

I interject, "I'm too tired to cook tonight. How about you get my card from my purse and order what you'd like. I don't have much of an appetite."

"Ok, but coach says we need to start eating homecooked meals. I thought we could do this meal together tonight. You know, I help you mix the meatloaf and prep the sides...like we used to do when..." he speaks but pauses abruptly.

"Liked we used to do when? You mean like we used to do when dad was alive?"

"Uh, well, yeah. We haven't done that since," he smiles, exposing his braces and dimples.

"No, I don't want to..."

"Ok, I'll just order something. I know you said you're not hungry, but I'll order you something just in case. Oh, yeah, don't worry about cleaning tonight, I've got it covered."

"Thank you, baby," I lean in, kissing him on the cheek.

He stands, heading toward the hallway with his gym bag.

"Oh, Mama?" Sean states, glancing back over his shoulder.

I raise my brows to acknowledge him.

"I have a game next Thursday. You think you can make it?"

"You know how I feel when I get off. Plus, you know I don't know a thing about basketball. Eric's dad is a much better participant than I, but I do love your stories over dinner when you finally make it home in the evenings," I smile slightly, yawning again.

Sean doesn't respond, he only walks away, but suddenly reappears again.

"You know what, no, this isn't right!"

Alarmed by his tone, I sit up, now at full attention.

"Excuse me?" I reply in a demanding manner.

"You never have time for me. You're always at work, if you're not there you're tired. You always have an excuse for not coming to my practices or games, and we rarely sit and eat together..."

"Now I don't know what the hell has gotten into you, but you better check yourself, young man! It's probably those boys you're hanging with!"

"See, that's just it, Mama. It's not them, it's you!"

Angered, I stand, placing my hands on either side of my waist.

"It's me? You have some damn nerve, Sean Anthony Bennett! I'm tired because I work to support this household, to support you and your wants and needs! Until you become an adult and assume some responsibilities, you have shit to say about anything! On top of everything else, I have to make time to visit your father and sister! What, have your balls dropped? You a man now?" I bellow, stepping closer to him with each word.

"But it is you, Mama! The sad part is, you can't see it! No disrespect, but you died when Samara did. You were hurt when Dad passed, but losing Samara only added the icing to the cake. You've been present, but your mind and soul are not in this house with you...with me! Since the day we got the news about Samara, the life, the spirit that once lived in you is gone. I look in your eyes and they're vacant, glazed over. As far as my balls, I don't exactly know what that means but I do know that I've had to step up and be the man in this house. Heck, I've become the parent. Our roles have reversed. I cook, clean, pay bills from your accounts, and get myself to and from school and practice. I do everything a man of the house, or a parent would do to keep us afloat. All this time, I've been here. I'm here, Mama! I'm right here!"

My jaw drops. I'm astounded by his words.

"Sean!"

"What?" he exclaims, throwing his hands in the air.

I look in my baby boy's eyes and see that he intended each word he uttered.

"How long have you felt this way?"

"Since Dad, but things went south after Samara passed," Sean clarifies.

And just like that, I realize what he's saying is true. It's all real and has been his reality for the last four years. From the age of eight to thirteen, my son, my baby boy has suffered. He's been alone, holding it down like the man that his father was raising him to be.

I pull Sean into my embrace, eagerly wanting to soak up his pain, hurt, loss, and confusion. All I can think to myself is how I not once considered how he was feeling. I was so wrapped up in grieving for myself that I didn't consider that he needed help grieving too.

CHAPTER 2

Things are still a bit awkward; Sean and I ride to church in silence. He's been quiet since Friday night, only speaking when necessary. I can't say that I blame him. I've got ground to make up. I must make things right with my son. I'm just a bit confused about how to do so. For quite some time, I've neglected him during one of the toughest situations he'll most likely have to endure in his lifetime.

My SUV rocks from side to side as we pull into the parking lot of the church and I waste no time shifting into the park.

"Sean, I wanted to..." I start to explain, but Sean hops out and closes the door before I can finish my sentence.

His best friend, Eric, just showed up. They've been joined at the hip since birth. I'll let him go and speak with him later.

———

"Good morning saints, welcome back. First Lady Gloria and I pray that each of you had a prosperous week. I've got a confession to make. I had a sermon planned out and last night God put it on my heart to change my sermon, that someone needed to receive a message today. I hope you all don't mind..."

"Speak, Pastor! Speak!" a random feminine voice echoes through the church from the congregation.

"Amen, Sista! Today's message is about grief. At some point in life, each of us will experience grief. The thing about experiencing grief is, each of us will experience it differently. There's no right or wrong way to experience it, as we are all unique in our emotions and feelings and how we go about expressing them. In your Bibles, turn to Matthew 11:28. Say Amen when you're there."

The congregation lets out scattered Amen's as everyone finds their place in the Bible for today's word.

"Matthew 11:28-30 reads, *Come to Me, all you who labor and are heavily laden, and I will give you rest. Take My yoke upon you and learn from Me, for I am gentle and lowly in heart, and you will find rest for your souls. For My yoke is easy and My burden is light.* The first thing you all should know and understand when faced with loss and grief is that it's ok to do so. We get so caught up in being strong, holding it together, that we forget something so simple...something...so...free...and liberating. I must admit, I'm guilty of this because this step is much easier said than done. When I lost my mother, I thought my world was ending. I detained all that anger and grief inside, knowing I wouldn't have my mother with me anymore. Thinking back now, I believe I didn't want to let it go because I felt as if I was letting *her* go. I was wrong. I leaned on my father, fasting and praying, asking God for answers, asking him for absolution. That night, my Bible fell open as I walked past it, slightly bumping it. It opened in the Book of Matthew. I sat and read that entire book that night, and I received the answers that I'd been praying for. Following God's word helped lead me to a peaceful place. This is not to say that I've forgotten my mother, but I've healed from her loss. I now feel that I can function. I no longer despised the memories I had of her, wishing she was here, but instead learned to cherish them. I learned to cherish the time we had. Folks, I won't sit here and say that this will happen overnight, but it can happen...if you allow it! God is waiting for you, with open arms, to aid you in taking on the pain you've been burdened with. He's here to provide you with the light you need after walking through a long, dark tunnel. He is salvation!" Pastor Henry speaks, nearly out of breath.

The congregation goes wild.

"If there is anyone in here today that's still holding on to some form of grief, come on down to the alter and start your healing process. Go ahead, take that first step."

Hesitant, I shift in my seat, looking around at others. Several have left their seats to head down to the altar. Pastor Henry keeps speaking, and like a bolt of lightning, something moves me. I'm up on my feet, making my way to the alter. I drop to my knees and close my eyes, placing my hands in position for prayer. I tune everyone out and whisper, speaking to the Lord, praying, begging him to help me find the healing I need to persevere. I need this, otherwise, I'm terrified I might lose my son in the process. Chills spread rampantly over my body, and I suddenly feel light as a feather.

"I got it," I cry out, waving my hands toward the heavens.

"Mama, you ok?" Sean questions, stepping to me in a panic.

I turn to my son, molding his face in my hands, stating, "Yes, everything is good now. I love you."

Not fully understanding the meaning behind my words, Sean

embraces me, murmuring, "I love you too."

———

"Good morning, Mrs. Bennett. How was your weekend?" the receptionist asks with an inviting smile.

"It was well, Chassidy, thanks for asking. How about you?" I return with a warm smile, signing in at the front desk.

We converse for a moment, sharing our life ventures since the last time we met, and I take a seat in the waiting area.

"Carissa Bennett," a familiar voice calls out.

I stand, grab my purse, and make a path to my next destination.

"Dr. Freeman, Mrs. Bennett is here for you," she opens the door, gesturing for me to enter.

"Thank you, Rayna," he nods.

Dr. Freeman stands at attention, greeting me.

"Please, have a seat, Mrs. Bennett. You look well."

Making myself comfortable, "Thank you, I feel well."

"Great. That's exactly what I'd like to hear," Dr. Freeman begins.

After Pastor Henry's sermon, I had a revelation about life in general, leading me to seek professional counseling. Honestly, it was a brilliant decision on my behalf, as I was in the process of completely losing myself and my son. For years I allowed the death of my husband and daughter to cast a shadow over my life, in turn leaving my son to receive the shitty end of the stick. I'm sure if I'd continued that path, sulking day after day, living in a past world filled with regret, guilt, and blame, my son would have grown to loathe and reject me. And like any mother who genuinely adores her children, I couldn't allow that to happen, I had to fight.

For the first time, I converse with Dr. Freeman, spilling my guts. In past sessions over the last few months, in Dr. Freeman's attempt to open me up he would ask questions, but my answers were nonchalant. The idea of speaking made me feel even more vulnerable than I did upon my first visit. Today is different, I feel uplifted and prepared to move forward. The usual hour session feels like five minutes today.

"I am grateful for today's appointment, as you've shown great stride in such a small timeframe. Now that we've opened a new door, now that you're more comfortable, I have homework for you."

"Homework?" I frown, not sure if I'm ready to hear what's next.

"Yes, homework," he nods. "This will be easy, and hopefully fun for you. In our past sessions, one major concern I had was your social life. You shut yourself off to the world after the loss of your husband and daughter. It's time you allow yourself to blossom again, to get out and do something for you..."

"Ok, like what?"

"Find something that you're particularly fond of, a hobby maybe? It could be a girl's night out for bowling or movies. Should you feel the need to ease yourself into it, go out alone. So long as you're outside of your comfort zones, work and home, it can be any activity you'd like. The overall goal is to be more social. Think you can pull this one off?"

"Yeah, I believe I can do that."

"Great! This concludes today's session. I want to see you

back in two weeks, and I expect a full report on your social time," Dr. Freeman grins, standing from his seat.

Dr. Freeman and I shake hands and he escorts me to the lobby to receive an appointment slip for my next visit. Chassidy provides me with my next appointment date and I head for the hallway to the elevator.

The elevator dings open, and I step inside, pressing P1 which leads to the underground parking garage where my vehicle is located. Just as the elevator doors prepare to meet, four fingers appear, and the doors separate, opening to reveal a middle-aged, solidly built Adonis.

"Going down?" he inquires.

"Uh, yeah...yes. Going down..." I mutter, fumbling over my words.

He nods, stepping inside, taking his place on the opposite side of the elevator.

The elevator jerks, kicking into motion and moving downward to P1. I've always had a fear of elevators, and my fear isn't relieved by the fact that the small space produces feelings of claustrophobia.

"You ok?" the brown eye stranger questions me with a look of concern.

"Not really. Elevators and I don't mix. I'll be happy when this thing stops," I exhale deeply, clutching my purse to relieve my anxiety.

"You know, I've never been a fan of them myself. I'd consider the stairs but the condition of my knees at my age won't allow it. So...elevator it is," he chuckles.

For a second, my anxiety subsides, and I crack a smile, loosening the grip on my purse. I can't help but admire the man standing before me. I don't believe I've seen anyone so handsome since my husband. Wait, on second thought, I may have but was blinded by my internal struggles.

Interrupting my lustful thoughts, the elevator jolts, coming to a screeching halt. Unsure of what's happening, I shriek, rushing myself into the back-left corner of the elevator. Careful not to fall, I widen my stance and open my arms, using my hands as a brace on the left and center back walls. Chin up and eyes closed, I attempt to steady my breathing.

"Hey, it's gonna be alright," the stranger in the elevator with me exclaims, grabbing hold of me.

In his grasp, I firmly take hold, wrapping my arms around his muscular body. With no warning, the elevator jolts again, dropping another story. I scream out, praying for help and mercy, considering we're on the sixteenth floor. He pulls me closer, easing me from the corner to the middle of the elevator.

"No, no, no!! What the hell are you doing?"

"It's ok," he immediately reassures me. "I'm going to use this call box here and phone for help. We're going to be fine..."

Someone answers the call and confirms that help has already arrived.

"See, someone's coming to help. They're going to stop this thing from moving. All we have to do is remain stationary, as the operator mentioned. Any small movement may cause the elevator to move again."

Still feeling unsafe, I only nod and close my eyes. Head against his chest, I can hear his heartbeat. He may be calm on the outside, but his heart says he's just as startled as I am by this ordeal.

"I know now is an awkward time for this, but I'm Reese."

"Carissa..." I reposition my arms, gripping him tighter than before.

Within minutes, we hear men rustling around on top of the elevator shaft. Then, the door is slowly pried open.

"Are the two of you ok? Is anyone injured?" a paramedic peeps through the opening.

The elevator is straddling the sixteenth floor and the wall beneath it. There's just enough room for two people to squeeze out at the same time.

"We are fine. The misses are just a bit shook up," Reese states winking at me.

The paramedic radios in and two others arrived to pull us out.

"Ladies first," Reese nods, crouching down and lifting me beneath my buttocks to boost me upward toward the opening.

Two paramedics grab both of my hands and pull me up, Reese giving one last push under the soul of my shoes to propel me out; Reese is pulled out next. We travel to the stairwell and are escorted down sixteen flights to the lobby. There, police and building management take our reports and contact information regarding the incident. After a thorough checkup by paramedics, Reese and I are released.

"Thank you for keeping me safe...and calm..." I shout awkwardly across the parking garage to Reese. He parked just a couple of rows over.

"Of course, you're welcome."

I step away from my car, walking another row over toward Reese.

"I owe you one..." I stutter, like a nervous schoolgirl.

"You don't owe me a thing. I'm just glad we both came out unharmed. That situation could have been more serious had the elevator fell any further."

I nod, walking back to my car. As I prepare to climb in, Reese's voice Grace's my ears.

"Since you're handing out IOUs, how about you do me the honor of taking you out for coffee. Starbucks?

"Uh...sure. Coffee's always good."

"How about right now?"

A bit shocked that he wants to go now, I'm left speechless.

With a slight chuckle, Reese grins, "I'll take that as a yes. Come on, follow me. There's a Starbucks about two or three blocks over."

Reese seats me and orders two Ice Caramel Macchiatos with our favorite desserts for us to devour at our leisure over the pleasant conversation. We converse about everything from family, religion, to politics in just under two hours.

"This was...I truly enjoyed myself...even though our meeting was through an awkwardly frightening encounter," Reese speaks warmly, politely taking my hands in his.

"Yes, I did as well. And although the circumstances were not usual, I wouldn't trade the encounter," I blush.

"Can I see you again? I enjoyed this meeting, but I'd like the opportunity to show you a much better time."

I want to say yes, but my body freezes. I don't know this man from Adam, I couldn't possibly go out on a date with him. As I fix my mouth to decline his offer, Dr. Freeman's voice resounds, reminding me of what I need to do to move forward.

"Sure."

"Whew, you had me for a minute. I thought you were going to say no."

We laugh wholeheartedly.

Reese retrieves a pen from his pocket and then flips my palm open. Just like back in the day, he writes his name and number in the palm of my hand. And just like a schoolgirl, I grin from ear to ear, blushing.

"Ms. Bennett, you enjoy the rest of your day," he bows, walking away.

In a faint voice, I reply, "You too...Mr. Thompson..."

CHAPTER 3

After working a 12-hour shift overnight at the hospital, I'm extremely worn and want nothing more than to crawl under my weighted comforter on this early Monday morning. Unfortunately, I can't. There's another pressing matter at hand. Knowing Sean is carpooling with his friend to school, I take a detour to the cemetery to visit Sam and Samara en route to my ultimate destination. I arrive downtown around 8:30 am, just early enough to be one of the first in line. Becoming drowsier by the minute, I wait impatiently in the lobby of an old, stale, rickety office building; waiting for my number to be called.

"Number 3!" a female voice calls out.

I look down at the small slip of paper in my hand. That's me, I'm number three. I gather my purse and key, approaching the window with my paperwork in hand. I hand the paperwork over to the young lady just on the other side of the window and she oddly glances at me. She asks that I wait a moment and steps away. Within seconds she reappears, along with an older, taller, robust gentleman.

"Good morning, ma'am. So, I understand that you want to submit a request for a name change to a street within this county. It appears you have the required documents to initiate the process. Could you tell me your reasoning behind requesting the change?"

I frown, but proceed, "Well, it's all there in the paperwork but I'm requesting the street be renamed after my daughter who passed a few years back. She was very influential, helping our youth and seniors, overall impacting the neighborhood and city until her death.

He examines the top paper through his bifocals and glares intensely.

"Samara...Bennett? That's your daughter?"

I nod.

"Ah, yes, I remember Ms. Bennett quite well. Ok, so at this point, your request will be submitted. It will then be scheduled to be included in an upcoming quarterly city council meeting. You'll receive a notice via mail of the hearing; the public will be notified as well to ensure their input before a decision is made..."

The gentleman, Mr. Graham, further explained the timeline in which it would be before I receive information regarding the hearing, the process, how to appeal, etc. The young lady provides me with a slip showing I submitted the paperwork; much like a timestamp. I thank them, grab my purse, and head for my vehicle.

One foot in front of the other, I walk swiftly, hurrying to get home to my bed. I usually don't work the night shift but a friend of mine took a vacation this week. Had it not been for the bond we created during our time in nursing school and the workplace,

I wouldn't have volunteered to do this. Getting off this time of morning makes me feel so out of place.

Making it to my vehicle, I prop my purse on the hood of the car, digging through to find my keys.

"Great!" I bellow, scaring a few birds away, realizing I'd left my keys in the building.

I scurry back in, looking around the now empty lobby for my keys. I spot them at the reception desk. Grabbing my keys, I take two steps toward the exit when I overhear Samara's name in conversation.

"I wish she'd just give up. You'd think that after we gave her a hard time in obtaining the application that she would have stopped. They're never going to reward her. For one, the situation surrounding her daughter's death will not stand. She flaunted around as if she was Martin Luther King, Jr. but was Malcolm X, teaching these other negroes to be volatile, disobedient, and combative. This will never stand..."

Making my presence known, I clear my throat as loudly as I can, allowing it to echo through the lobby. The young lady and gentleman that I'd originally spoken with lookup, like a deer looking into headlights. From the look in their eyes alone, I can assume they expected to be alone and didn't anticipate I'd overhear their thoughts surrounding Samara.

"I want you two to know that I heard every word that you said, and should anything go wrong with this, you will hear from me. Like a lioness does to feed her young, I will hunt you down and chew you to itty bitty pieces. You'll be begging for me to let up, you'll be begging for my forgiveness and God's mercy..." I state firmly, in the lowest voice possible, gritting my teeth.

They sit staring back at me, looking like the fools they are.

I don't wait for a response, I whip around, charging for the front door. I know that there are still racist individuals in this town, on this earth, but I didn't expect the people handling my paperwork to hold such opinions. NO matter how hard we try, there will always be someone, somewhere who doesn't approve of what we do or who we are simply because we're black.

————

I'm awakened by a piercing voice and violent shaking. Unaware of my surroundings, I fight back, swinging my arms in any direction possible before fully opening my eyes.

"Mama! Stop fighting! It's me! It's Sean!" he screams, taking blow after blow from my fists.

Heart racing, I manage to focus my vision, realizing that Sean's standing over me.

"Sean, goodness, you scared the hell out of me. Why were you screaming and yelling at me? You know I've been at work all night..." I hold my chest, trying my best to slow my breathing.

"I'm sorry, Mama, I'm just excited. Look what came in the mail today!"

He forks over papers. Scanning them, I comprehend what all the fuss is about. At 13, he's been invited to attend a summer league for up-and-coming student-athletes. They only accept a limited number of students a year, so the fact that he was selected is a very big deal.

Sean and I hold hands, yelping for joy. I can't remember the last time we'd been this happy...together.

"We should celebrate! Let me get myself together and we can go anywhere you'd like for dinner..." I loosen my grip on his hands.

"You know, I was thinking that we could stay in...maybe cook

our dinner? It's been a while since we've done that...together..."
Sean answers shyly, looking away.

I take a moment to examine his stature, his body language.
He almost looks scared to ask. My poor baby.

To reassure him, I lift his chin in my hand, looking him right
in the eyes, "Of course, we can. We can do whatever you'd like
sweetie. Just say the words."

He doesn't waste a second, running out of my bedroom and
down the hallway to his.

———

Sean and I patrol every aisle of the grocery store for the
ingredients required for his choice of dinner. I don't know if this
meal choice has suddenly become his favorite meal, but I don't
find it to be a coincidence that he wants his father's favorite
meal: Meatloaf, cabbage, macaroni and cheese, cornbread, and
homemade lemonade. The meal sounds simple, and it is, but it
was Sammie's favorite to have. I don't say a word about Sean's
dinner plans, I just go along, agreeing to purchase whatever he
needs to create and make this meal his own.

Sean gleams with joy as we head for the register. Most of the
registers are full, having at least four people in line, but we
manage to find a line with only two people in front of us.

"Looks like we might be awhile..." Sean sighs.

"Why do you say that?" I inquired, looking up from my
phone.

I'm addicted to Candy Crush and must play every chance I
get. I've been telling myself that I use it as a distraction from my
reality, but the truth is I'm addicted to it like most people who
play.

"The lady upfront, her card isn't working. Maybe we should move to another line?"

Leaning to the left, I see a young lady, no older than 25, in conflict with the cashier. Her card won't approve and she's doing everything she can to explain to the cashier that there's a balance on the card and it's active. Despite her efforts, there's nothing the cashier can do at this point but hold or cancel the transaction.

I look at the gentleman standing only inches from the end of our buggy, and his body language suggests he's beyond irritated.

"Babe let's give it a few more minutes, and if we need to move, we will..." I sound, and the gentleman turns about, looking me square in the eye.

To my surprise, it's a familiar face.

"Well, isn't it a small world," Reese states, giving Sean and me a warm smile.

"Indeed, it is. How are you?"

"Just trying to pick up some grocery but it doesn't look as if I'll get to use it. I've been standing here for right at ten minutes..." he speaks a bit louder, just loud enough so the young lady with the cashier can hear.

She cuts her eyes our way and rolls them.

Changing the conversation, I ask, "How's life been treating you? Anything interesting? You haven't gotten stuck on any elevators lately have you?"

Reese chuckles, "Thank goodness, no! I don't think I could handle another event like that anytime soon. My nerves and patience aren't what they once were."

I nod in agreement. I can completely appreciate his sentiments in that area, as I find myself short on nerves and patience in my line of work. I take a moment to introduce Sean and

Reese. I snicker at Sean's behavior. Upon introduction, Sean immediately straightens his back and broadens his shoulders, shaking Reese's hand firmly. I find it hilarious because he's acting like a typical man, sizing Reese up. I guess that's fair, as he's been the man of the house since his father passed on. The two chat for a minute but that's short-lived.

The store manager comes over, attempting to suspend the order, but by now Reese is riled up.

"You see, if these young people would quit living off the government and get a job, this wouldn't be an issue. If you're going to mooch off the government, at least make sure your benefits are working..." he scoffs, throwing his hand basket onto the conveyor belt.

Sean and I glance at one another, probably sharing the same thoughts, but don't say anything further.

"I need to step outside and take a phone call, but I do want the groceries," I overhear the young lady's voice to the manager.

"It's probably not even her card...probably bought stamps off of someone...that's why the card won't work properly..." Reese snaps, causing everyone in the store to have eyes on our lane.

A bit shocked, I decide to intervene, "Reese, hey, it's ok."

Lowering his tone, Reese replies, "No, it's not ok. She's up in here with pajamas on, a bonnet, and house shoes. The white man already thinks we ain't shit. Her coming in here dressed like that and her EBT card's not working only proves what they've suggested about us for years. I hate to see folks abusing the system, then blaming it on "repression" when they can't get where they want in life. We're all afforded the same opportunities..."

I quickly work to quiet him down; his voice is ascending again.

The young girl's transaction is suspended and within a few minutes, Sean and I can check out and be on our way.

"What was that all about?" Sean asks as we put the last of the bags into the back of the car.

I just shake my head. I have no idea what got into Reese. I've only met him once before, not talking to him since we parted at Starbucks some weeks back.

Sean closes the hatch on my car and heads over to a buggy rack on the row over from where we're parked.

"Hey, I just want to apologize for my behavior in there. It's been a long week and it's only Tuesday..." Reese speaks softly, hands in his pocket, eyes to the ground like a child in trouble.

"As you should be. You don't know that young lady's situation. She could really need help to feed her children or herself. You don't know her need and you judged her, not knowing her circumstances. Sometimes what we see isn't always what it seems...if that makes sense. So, you shouldn't be apologizing to me. You should be apologizing to her..."

"You're right, and I did. I caught her before she left the parking lot and apologized for my behavior."

I don't reply, left feeling a bit awkward by the entire situation.

Breaking the silence, Reese changes the subject, "I haven't heard from you. Did you lose my number?" he asks, taking the hand he'd written his number in a few weeks back.

"No, I didn't lose it. I've just been...busy..."

"Understandable. Carissa, I'd like to see you again, to get to know you better..."

I nod, trying not to give in too easily, especially after his behavior in the store. As Sean heads back to the vehicle, Reese leans in, whispering warm, sweet nothings into my ear. The deepness of his voice alone sets me afire, causing me to giggle like a teenage girl who's just run into her crush.

"So, dinner, us, tomorrow?"

"Deal," I grin bashfully.

"Sean, you have a good day!" Reese waves before heading to his truck.

In a trance, I stand in the exact spot where Reese left me as he drives by, honking as he passes. As the sound of his truck's motor fades, I snap out of my trance and hop into the car.

"What was that all about?" Sean quizzes.

"It was nothing..."

"Oh, that was definitely nothing..." he jokes, staring me down from the passenger seat.

"Alright...alright. I may like him...a little...a little," I express to Sean, with emphasis on "a little". "What do you think about him? I saw you sizing him up."

"I mean, he seems clean-cut and about his business, *but* he was a little weird in the grocery store. Outside of that, I think he's okay...but I still need to know more about him. I can't have my Mama out here with just anyone."

The look on his face tells me that Sean's serious about me seeing other people. What I respect most is that my attraction to Reese doesn't seem to bother Sean. It feels as if he's ok with me working to move forward and find happiness, even if it's with another man who's not his father.

———

As agreed, Reese and I go out on a date. Instead of the usual, he surprises me with a picnic at a popular park in town. With a blanket, some white wine, and finger foods, we sit out and enjoy one another's company. Reese is so attentive to my needs, asking all the right questions, doing all the right things.

"Are you enjoying yourself?" Reese inquires as we stare into the sunset.

"Oh, definitely. It's been some time since I've genuinely enjoyed the company of another since…" I pause, afraid to say what's on my tongue.

"It's ok to say it. Don't be ashamed of losing your husband, of being a widow. I'm not ashamed to say that I'm divorced. I know these are two different situations, but I've grown from the experience."

I tear up a bit because recently I've been struggling with moving on, as moving on might indicate that I've forgotten about Sam or no longer love him. It feels good to have another adult express their feelings regarding their relationship, admit their wrongdoings, and move on with life. Above all, I respect Reese's honesty.

"If I haven't already done so, I want to show my gratitude. I appreciate you taking the time out to do this with me today. This feels good…" Reese begins, but I interrupt, "It feels right…"

He nods, smiling, placing his hand over mine.

Unannounced, Reese leans in, slightly pressing his lips against mine. I soften my composure, fully taking him into him. He reaches around and grabs me around the waist, pulling me closer, causing the blanket underneath us to gather. For the first time in forever, I feel…emotion, affection.

As our lips release, I catch a glimpse of the time on my phone.

"Oh, my God! I'm late! I'm late, I gotta run," I hop up like Cinderella, nearly losing one of my sandals.

"I've been calling you! Where have you been? I've been worried!"

"I'm here...I'm here..." I stumble into Wednesday night bible study nearly half an hour late, ignoring Sean's interrogation.

I quietly settle down and unpack my study book so that I may join in. As always, First Lady is delivering a thought-provoking message. Tonight's read is from Proverbs 28:13:

Whoever conceals his transgressions will not prosper, but he who confesses and forsakes them will obtain mercy.

I follow First Lady's message for the next half hour, and we end this week's bible study session.

"You doing alright, Sista Bennett? I saw you flying in here last minute."

"Yeah, just lost track of time," I answer shamefully, knowing that I was busy becoming acquainted with a handsome stranger.

"It happens to the best of us..." Pastor Henry begins but I intervene saying, "Pastor, may I speak with you about something?"

He nods.

"You know I've been in a rough place since Sam and Samara passed away, and I've finally taken on the skills I need to cope. I've met someone, and I want to know should I do this? Have I given myself enough time to heal?"

"There's no set timeframe for healing, we all heal differently. How well do you know this person?"

"We're newly acquainted but there's a connection. If I may be honest, I'd like to see where it goes. I think I owe myself that. I want to feel again..."

"That's understandable. Just be mindful of the company you keep. You know, the Lord sometimes brings folks into our lives for a reason and sometimes a season. Not everyone is meant to be permanent; some are temporary. You're still in a vulnerable stage, so be careful.

I frown a bit, inwardly questioning Pastor Henry's statement. He's right, I'm still vulnerable but I owe it to myself. I deserve happiness. Right?

CHAPTER 4

Since I last spoke with Pastor Henry, the words he left me with have been lingering like the pain of a stumped toe. Worsening matters, I've had vivid, recurring dreams of snakes. I recall having my first snake dream around the age of 15. The dream startled me awake, inducing screams and labored breathing. My grandmother rushed in, comforting me, asking me what was wrong. I explained my dream and her response was immediate.

I'll never forget, as an eerie feeling that I hadn't felt before possessed my tiny, teenage frame.

Holding me by my wrists with her soft, wrinkled hands, she glares, "Child, a dream like this can only mean one thing; there is an enemy in your circle. You need to be mindful, watch, and stay prayed up. Do these things and God will point out and remove them from your life, knowingly or unknowingly."

I nodded my head, not fully understanding what my grandmother meant. Honestly, I thought she was a bit crazy, but I took her words and held on to them. Three weeks later, one of my close friends and I were in the gymnasium alone and she began to say some weird things. I gave her a weird look and she then proceeded to throw me into the boy's locker room, locking me inside. I yelled and screamed, banging on the door. Two boys, seniors on the basketball and football teams, appeared from nowhere and crept toward me. One held me down while the other ripped my clothes away from my body, prying my legs apart. Just as I thought I was done for, that my innocence was about to be robbed, the basketball coach broke the lock and burst into the locker room. Needless to say, I had a clear understanding of my grandmother's words at that moment. My so-called friend and the two guys were tried and convicted. They've all since been released from jail and fell into other troubles, landing them back behind bars. After this incident at 15, I only had one other occurrence of a snake dream which was in college. Turns out, my college roommate was hoarding drugs. I received a notice that I was being relocated to another dorm and the following day my roommate was busted for drug possession and distribution. Since then, I've learned to take heed to these sorts of dreams.

Pastor Henry fell ill before I was able to speak with him again. So, along with Pastor Henry's words and my dreams, who in my life do I need to watch out for? Reese is the only person to recently enter my life, so it can't be him. Come to think of it, since Samara's death, I'd have a plethora of individuals reach out, one tried to scam people with a GoFundMe account. Here recently I've had a group of individuals reach out, wanting to further Samara's cause. I was suspicious of them to start but welcomed their ideas to further what Samara had started. I don't know who the culprit is, but based on past experiences with these dreams, God will reveal them. I do not doubt that.

———

"What are you doing over there?" Sean quizzes, looking back at me over his left shoulder.

"Oh, nothing. Cooking..." I giggle, not looking up from my phone.

For the last three months, Sean and I have devoted our undivided attention to one another. We've only done home-cooked meals and outings on the weekend that interest us both like basketball, bowling, movies, laser tag, etc. At 50, and considering I have a demanding career, I didn't realize I still possessed this amount of energy. I can truly say that Sean has returned my youthfulness. And right on time too, might I add. Not only have Sean and I strengthened our bond, but so have Reese and I. We've been on dates almost weekly, and we've even done a mini-vacation. Overall, we've become more acquainted, learning more about one another. Honestly, I think I've revealed a little more about myself than I normally would, but he's so easy to converse with. It may sound weird, but I feel as if I've known him forever. With Reese, I feel safe...I feel...comfortable.

"Oh, you're not cooking because the veggies you're sautéing are nearly burnt," Sean exclaims, dropping his cooking utensils to rescue the portion of dinner I'm responsible for preparing.

I hate to admit, but Sean's right. I haven't paid the food any attention, my attention is on the text messages flowing in. Texting has never been my forte but since Reese and I met, texting has been a method of contact for us. The crazy part is, Sean's been working aimlessly to help me learn the ins and outs of text messaging, but it's taken a handsome man to convert me in that department.

"Is that who I think it is?" Sean huffs, rolling his eyes.

Lifting my eyes from the screen, in a curious manner I reply, "I don't know. Who do you think it is?"

Sean gives me this look. That's all the indication I need. He knows exactly what I'm doing.

"You're the mom, you make the rules, but I just have to say I've never seen you this way. You're..."

"I'm what!" I snap, not giving him a chance to finish his sentence.

"Whoa, partner, slow your roll," he jokes, holding both his hands in the air. "I'm just saying I've never seen you so smitten before. I remember things with you and Dad but those memories, unfortunately, have started to fade. I find myself not remembering how he sounds anymore. Over the last two years, I've found myself watching old birthday videos just to hear his and Samara's voices. You look happy Mama. Knowing you're happy is all I need right now..."

My baby boy sounds like a man. For the first time in nearly 45 minutes, I lay my phone down and walk over to my son, taking him into my arms. As I did when he was younger, I speak a baby talk to him, and shower him with kisses.

"Ma! You gotta stop. I'm not two anymore," Sean pushes me away, frowning up.

"Well, just so you know, I don't care if you're two or twenty-two, you'll always be my baby..."

"I love you, Mama..."

"I love you, too, baby. Now, let's finish this dinner before our company arrives and nothing is complete."

Sean nods and we get to work. For the next two hours, we converse and cook, cleaning along the way.

Time flies and I overhear the doorbell chime.

"I got it," Sean yelps, removing his apron and paving his way to the front door.

Dinner is practically complete, I'm just working to plate the cake I've baked. I pull out the crystal cake plate that my mother gifted Sam and me on our wedding day and remove it from the bunt pan.

Sean escorts Reese into the kitchen.

"Hello, beautiful..." Reese smiles, roses in hand, leaving me with a kiss on the cheek.

"Roses? You shouldn't have!"

"Anything to see you smile. So, tell me, why are you still in here cooking? You didn't have to do all this. I could have paid for us to go out. You know I don't mind."

"I know you don't mind, but you can't get on to me this time. This was all Sean's idea. "He's the one that wanted to stay in and cook dinner tonight..." I give Reese the side-eye.

"Is something wrong with my wanting to stay in and cook?"

"Oh, not at all. You know, I've gotta say, you have an old soul," Reese tells Sean, patting him on the back.

"Old soul?"

"Yes, that just means you're beyond your years. Come on, let's talk..." Reese leads Sean toward the living room, leaving me with a wink.

As I clear out and add the remaining dishes to the dishwasher, I listen in on Sean and Reese's conversation.

"So, my Mom tells me you're retired military and law enforcement?" Sean strikes up the conversation.

Lord, the man hasn't been here an hour and he's already quizzing him.

With no hesitation, Reese obliges, elaborating on his time in the military and his time as an officer. Outside of sports and cooking, Sean's always wanted to join the military.

As they continue, I place the meal Sean and I have prepared down the center of the dining table, putting out my best china and silverware.

Just as I place the last napkin, I overhear Sean, "...but that's gone now. You know, it's been difficult for my Mom since my father and sister passed..."

I lower my head, cocking it to the side, much like an antenna, making sure that I hear everything.

"So, your mother told me that she'd lost her husband and daughter. She told me about your father, Sam, but she never really talks about your sister. What happened?" Reese probes.

"Dinner is ready!" I shout, purposely clanging one of the glasses against a plate.

Although Reese and I have been talking for months, sharing details about Samara is not something I'm ready to speak on just yet. I've even removed all pictures of her and Sam from my living space. I couldn't bear to look upon their faces day after day, feeling as if I'd failed them, as if there was more I could have done to save them both. Plus, people would come over to visit Sean and me, and somehow, we'd end up in deep conversation about Samara and Sam, how beautiful they were when they were alive. To quit reliving those talks repeatedly, I removed the pictures. Their pictures are put away in Samara's room, which is safe behind locked and key. I've even talked with my therapist about it and he agrees that I should wait until I'm comfortable.

———

"Dinner was absolutely amazing. You two did an amazing job. I know where to come when I need a decent meal in this town," Reese utters, leaning back in his chair, rubbing his gut in satisfaction.

"We'd love to have you again..." I smile, trying not to display how giddy I am.

"Hey, Mom, do you mind if I spend the weekend with Eric. I've already cleared my stay with his Dad."

Noting Sean's eagerness, I nod, and he jumps up almost instantly.

"Reese, it was great to officially meet you tonight. I learned much more from you than I anticipated..." Sean begins, leaving Reese with a firm, manly handshake.

It takes Sean no time to pack an overnight bag and roll out.

"Well, that didn't take long. He got outta here in a jiffy, didn't he?"

"Yeah, that's normally how it is. He loves time with me, but I can never beat the company his best friend offers him."

"Whoa, let me take care of that for you," Reese steps in, removing some dishes from my hands.

"Oh, it's fine, I got it," I speak, but Reese is adamant, stating, "After all you two did tonight to make this dinner a success, clearing the table and loading your dishwasher is the least I could do..."

"It's just been a while since I had an actual man around the house helping with anything. It's just been Sean and I..." I look away, twiddling my thumbs.

"That's understandable, but I'm here now, and so long as the two if you will have me, I'm not going anywhere."

My heart sinks and a smile shines through. Lord knows how

long I've waited to hear those words. It's good to know that Sean and I have someone that we can count on.

Just as I put away the last of the kitchen utensils, and I hear faint jazz music coming from the living room. Normally I only listen to my jazz collection when I'm cleaning or drinking my wine. I drop what I'm doing and walk into the living room. There I find Reese dancing, in his world, unaware of me admiring his moves.

He extends his hands, wine glasses in both, gesturing I join him in dancing. I approach, taking one of the wine glasses into my hand.

"You got the moves, huh?" Reese laughs, pulling me in by my waist.

The feel of his hands groping my midsection is surely a sensation that hasn't been present in many moons.

"I don't know if I've told you this, but you are mighty beautiful tonight."

I snicker but my smile quickly fades as I realize Reese is being serious.

"Well, you're quite handsome yourself," I comment, suddenly in a trance by his honey-colored eyes.

Reese gulps the remainder of his wine down and presses his lips against mine. Nearly dropping my wine glass, I indulge in Reese, kissing him passionately.

The flame I've been so determined to suppress has been awakened.

"I'm sorry, I shouldn't..."

Reese halts all action and pulls away from me.

"Wait, what's wrong?"

"I don't want to rush things. We've only been seeing one another for a few months, but I care for you deeply. I don't want

to let my emotions or impulsiveness have you ruin the relationship that we've built this far. If my previous marriage and separa-
tion from my children taught me anything, it's to learn from my
previous mistakes."

I nod and agree with his reasoning, but deep down I have a
burning desire for Reese.

"I think it is best I leave...before I do something I regret..."

Reese thanks me once again for a wonderful evening, kisses
me on my right cheek, and disappears beyond my front door.

I down my wine in one swallow and walk the glasses to the
kitchen, placing them into the sink.

The doorbell sounds.

I shuffle to the front door and open it. It's Reese. Before I
can respond, ask him if he's left something, he takes me into his
arms, closing the door with his foot. He leads me to the couch,
kissing me all the while.

"I can't leave you..." he utters passionately between breaths.

"Then don't..." I moan.

Breathing heavily, Reese stares me dead in the eyes and now
I know exactly what I want. I take him by the hand, leading him
down the hallway to my master suite.

Like a couple teenagers, we wrestle with one another,
removing clothes, slinging them across the room. Reese kisses
me tenderly down the right side of my neck, trailing down to my
shoulder blades. He asks for my permission and I grant it, lifting
me from the floor onto my bed, lightly pressing my thighs apart
and nestling his thickly built frame between mine.

Reese enters, and the magic starts, sending waves of tingling
sensations through my body. I bury my freshly manicured nails
into his back, attempting to fight off the urge to ejaculate
prematurely. As appealing as it sounds to release now, I haven't

been with a man in years and I want nothing more than to savor this moment.

Reese becomes more in tune with our sexual encounter, breathing intensely, gripping and biting any flesh of mine that his mouth can reach. Reese tightens his grip on my body, moaning, and then he states the unexpected, "I...I love you, Carissa. Please....be mine."

My body tenses, quivering slightly, and my insides cream to the words "I love you."

———

I wake to a bump. It's Reese, he's getting dressed to leave.

"Are you leaving?" I inquire, sitting up in bed.

"I...I was going to...yes..." he admits.

"So, you're just going to have sex with me and leave? We're not teenagers, Reese."

"No. No, baby, it's not like that. I just didn't want to wear out my welcome. Do you want me to stay?"

I pause, taking a second to think things through.

I extend my hand and softly reply, "Stay with me..."

Reese quickly undresses and climbs into bed, snuggling my body to his. I was once a believer that I'd only find one soulmate in my life. Now I'm convinced the Lord's granted me two.

CHAPTER 5

J ust under five months have passed since I submitted the street name request to the city council, but I've yet to receive anything in the mail regarding a public hearing as the gentleman at the office downtown stated I would. Considering what I'd overheard while there, I left feeling uneasy but decided I should allow those individuals to do their job. I'm all for giving chances until people prove otherwise.

"Sean..." I call out, walking through the front door from a grocery store run.

Along with Eric, Sean files into the living room, "Yes, ma'am."

"Oh, I didn't realize you had company. I just wanted to talk with you for a moment."

"Oh, no worries, Mrs. C. I was just on my way out. Sean and I were discussing some sports-related stuff and some things we'd seen on the news. You doing ok?"

"Yes, Eric. I'm doing fine. Tell your folks hello for me."

Eric exits, and I return my attention to Sean.

"Has any mail come in from the city council?"

"No, ma'am, but I'll check the stack on the computer desk just to be safe. Is something wrong?" Sean asks, flipping through the mail.

I explain that I'm waiting for the public hearing notice from the city council regarding the street name change, that I should have received it already. Sean and I work together to find the paperwork but come up empty-handed.

"So, what do we need to do now?"

"Oh, I'm going down there. I know for sure they've already had this meeting, they just excluded me from the agenda. Considering it's Friday, I want to get down there early to see what the issue is. Would you like to ride?"

"Uh, I was wondering if I could go shoot ball with Eric and some other guys from school. We'll be down at Trevor's house, about two blocks over from here."

"Trevor Johnson?"

"Yes. Do you mind? But if you want me to go with you, I don't mind."

"No, no, I can handle it. Just get the ok from his parents and I will drop you there on my way out."

———

Spring and Summer fade, late fall is upon us. The sunrise from this morning has faded and clouds have set in, causing it to be a bit cooler than normal for this time of year. While waiting for Sean, I grab a light jacket from the hall closet and head for the car. A couple of minutes pass and Sean comes out, locking the door behind him, wearing an all-back hoodie and carrying a black duffle bag. He throws his bag into the backseat and climbs into the front with me.

"You know I don't like for you to wear those hoods over your head. When you're out and about, be sure to keep that thang off your head..." I state, pulling out of the driveway.

"It's cool out, Mama. I had to throw something on to cover my ears for the moment."

"I get that, but you know the stigma behind these hoodies and things. I don't want you to get caught up in anything. You hear?"

Sean nods. He's probably tired of hearing me talk about this topic. Frankly, I don't care. I'm just doing my due diligence, keeping him safe. Within a couple minutes, we're at Trevor's house and I confirm with his mother that Sean is clear to stay. Sean takes his bag from the backseat and comes around to the driver's side to say bye.

"Hey, hoodie, take it off your head. Put your beanie on if you need to but keep that hoodie off your head."

"Ma, c'mon!"

"Dammit, Sean, do as I say! Take the damn hoodie off..." I grit, gripping the steering wheel.

"Ok, ok, I get it. I get it. It's coming off..." he mumbles.

"Do you? Do you get it, Sean?"

"Yeah..."

"What do you get?"

"Trayvon Martin..."

"It's so much more than Trayvon! Yes, Trayvon lost his life for no reason while wearing a hoodie, Sean, but he was profiled for what he was wearing...for the way that he looked...the color of his skin...because he was perceived as a damn threat! So, the next time

I ask you to remove that damn hoodie from your head, you think about Trayvon, Tamir Rice, Eric Garner, and all the other young men and women...they lost their lives or innocence and should serve as an example for you as a young black man. Understood?"

A bit shaken, Sean's demeanor stiffens. He only nods at what I've stated.

———

I arrive downtown only to find the office that I'd gone to a few months ago is being remolded and there doesn't seem to be another address posted stating they're working from another location. I call several numbers, only to end up leaving a voicemail.

I meet with my therapist for an hour, receive good feedback and yet another homework assignment, and meet with a coworker for some bargain shopping. After arriving at the third department store, I finally decide I'd purchased enough clothes, maybe some shoes and jewelry are the better options. We approach the register for checkout and my phone buzzes. I retrieve my phone from my purse; it's a news report.

I turn down the volume on my phone and open the news link; it's live.

"What's that you're watching?" my coworker questions, handing her department store card to the cashier.

"My goodness! It looks as if a riot broke out downtown...on the Southside..." I mutter, squinting to see the footage on my 6.5-inch phone screen.

"A riot? Since when? Who's orchestrating it!?"

"I have no idea, but from the footage, I see there's a gang of people down there..."

"Lord, have mercy! When will these folks learn? It's one thing to protest, but to riot? And in our area? They are all aware that part of town has nothing but black-owned businesses and whatnot. If you wanna riot, don't tear up your shit!"

"I agree..." I sigh, not shying away from the feed.

My phone buzzes again; this time it's a phone call. It's my neighbor, Mr. Sandoval, telling me that I need to look at the news. He's an elderly gentleman who lives alone just two doors down from my place. He's was much like a grandfather figure to my family.

"Mr. Sandoval, I'm viewing on my phone right now. Are you ok?"

"Yes, but you need to look closer. Sean is out there! He's in a black hoodie..." Mr. Sandoval further explains.

Sean is out there!

Mr. Sandoval's voice echoes through my entirety, creating a chill down to my bones.

"I gotta go!" I scramble, dropping the clothes and jewelry I'd draped over my right arm while shopping.

"Wait, what's wrong?"

"Sean's out there at this damn riot!"

My coworker stalls, looking directly into my eyes. It's at that moment I realize we're both thinking the same thing.

"Go...go! I'll catch an Uber back to my car. Just keep me posted on what's happening."

No time to speak, I throw my left hand up, running out of the department store and out to my vehicle.

———

I arrive on the Southside and it's only a sight that I've seen in movies. There are police cars, ambulances, fire trucks, and pedestrians in every direction. I park in the lot of a strip mall about a block down and power walk north toward the action.

There are people everywhere, some with concealed carry weapons on their hips, pepper spray, or other objects like rocks, box cutters, etc., in their hands as they chant. Feeling as if I'm lost in a sea of darkness, I turn in ninety-degree increments peeling the crowd for my son. I spot him across the crowd with Eric.

Like an enraged bull, I plow through the crowd with tunnel vision. As I approach Sean, I loosen my fist, spreading my fingers out as far as they can go, palm open. I sneak up from behind and...*SMACK!*

In a sweeping motion, I take my hand across the back of Sean's head, knocking the black hood from his head.

"Damn!" he screeches, turning to find I'm standing behind him.

"Oh, you're cursing now?" I grit, punching him in the arm.

"Mama! What are you doing? Why are you hitting me?" he ducks and dodges me, dropping a huge rock from his hand

"For the same reason, your ass is out here and not at Trevor's place as you said you'd be! And what the hell are your plans with this rock? You going to hit someone or something with it? And I see you still have this damn hoodie over your head when I directly instructed you not to!" I push and punch him more.

Every fiber of my being is ignited with anger. I can't believe Sean would do something like this. He's smarter than this!

I yell and punch Sean as he makes a run for it, most likely embarrassed that I'm dragging him away from the riot. He makes a break for it, running down the street. I may be 50, but

I've still got life left in me. I run right behind him, catching up to him, screaming and shouting all the while. We finally make it to the car, and he hops inside, slamming the door. His slamming my car door pisses me off more.

"Sean, what the hell has gotten into you? Why are you down here?" I ask furiously, driving off like a bat out of hell.

With a frown taking over his face, he mutters, "Just supporting the cause Mama..."

"And what cause is that? Do you even know? Huh?"

He shrugs.

"I didn't think you did! You're just following the crowd!"

"I'm not just following anyone, Mama, I came with Eric..." he speaks again, but I interrupt stating, "Eric is far from a good experience, you know this, but somehow you keep allowing him to influence you."

"Eric didn't influence my coming. I came on my own accord, Mama."

"So, you support rioting?"

"No, ma'am, just wanted to show my support for all the negative things that have happened to black people lately."

I pull into my driveway and put the car in park. My mind is all over the place, my heart is pounding a mile a minute.

My ringer goes off, it's Reese.

"Go in the house, I'll be in to talk with you in a minute..."

"Yes, ma'am..." Sean drops his head between his shoulders, climbing out of the front seat.

I answer Reese's phone call and he's in a panic. He tells me that he caught live footage of me dragging Sean away from the riot. He's sending me screenshots of comments from various social media outlets. They're naming me a "hero", "Mom of the Year", and other things that I don't feel that I am. I was simply doing what I needed to do to protect my son from the same fate as my daughter. Still, a bit overwhelmed by the entire ordeal, Reese offers to stop by; I agree.

Reese arrives in no time, ringing the doorbell. I answer, pleased to see him, but he blows right by me and heads directly for Sean. I want to go in and watch them talk, but something tells me that Sean needs a man right now, so I pace the living room floor twiddling my thumbs. I listen in as much as I can, but I can only hear words sparingly.

Just as I decide to sit on the loveseat and attempt to calm my nerves, Sean and Reese appear.

"Now apologize to your mother..." Reese states firmly, patting Sean on the back.

Sean approaches me, taking my hands in his, letting out a tear-filled apology as I've never heard in my 50 years of living.

"Apology accepted."

"I'll never do that again, Mama, I swear. I didn't mean to hurt you..."

"See, that's the thing, Sean. You didn't hurt me. When I saw you out there with that hoodie on and that rock in your hand, my mind immediately went left. All I could imagine was what *could* have happened. You could have been hurt, even killed, in that mess out there. I won't stand for it. If I lose you, I have no one else. I know we all have a time here on this earth, but I won't allow this to be the way your time here with me is ended. I've already lost one child to violence, I refuse to lose you too. I won't bury another child before the good Lord calls me home...I can't..." I begin to sob, tears streaming from my eyes down onto my cheeks.

"You won't lose me, Mama, I'm sure of it. I'll never put myself in that position again."

I nod, taking him into my arms as tightly as the day that he first entered this world.

Sean loosens his grip and I let go, allowing him to turn to Reese.

"Reese, thank you for coming by. It's been a while since I had a father, a man, around to talk to, to get me level. My mom is doing her very best but having a male figure to look up to means everything to me. So, thank you, for being here not just for my mom but for me."

"I wouldn't have it any other way. C'mon, bring it in," Reese smiles, opening his arms to hug us both.

For the first time in a long time, *both* Sean and I can add a missing piece to this puzzle we call life.

CHAPTER 6

I wake to a dark, rainy Sunday morning in the arms of the man who's recently stolen my heart. After Sam, I thought I'd never be able to love again. Truth is, I was afraid to love again, thinking I'd be letting Sam go...letting our years of love go. Still seeing my therapist and occasionally Pastor Henry, I've learned this is not the case. There's room in our hearts for more than one great love in a lifetime.

As I lie awake, watching Reese rest, his eyes begin to flutter open.

"Good morning, beautiful," he grins, yawning.

"Hey, handsome, about time you wake. I was nearly tired of being alone."

"Well, I'm here now. Something bothering you?"

"No, I just need you..." I reply softly, running my fingertips down the center of his chest to his navel.

"Alright now, you're going to awaken the beast," he winks.

"Maybe I want to..." I tease, rolling on top of Reese, grinding my center on his.

He smiles wickedly, clasping his hands around my bare waist. He knows what time it is.

———

"Something smells good..." Sean yawns, walking into the kitchen.

"Yeah, I decided to do an entire spread. Hope you're ready to grub this morning."

"Always," Sean kisses me on the cheek. "You know, Mom, it's good to see you like this again. You look...happy."

"That's because I am happy, baby, for the first time in a while. Are you happy though? No matter what's happening in my world, you come first..." I ask, dropping the pancake spatula to give Sean my undivided attention.

"Oh, definitely, more than ever here lately. So, I see Reese's car outside? Is he here?"

I cringe at Sean's question. Not that he isn't aware of my relationship with Reese, but Reese and I have done a great job with him being gone before the day; making sure he doesn't stay over too long or too often. How do I answer Sean? I guess the only way is to answer with honesty.

"Yes, he's here..." I respond cautiously, looking away shamefully.

"Cool."

"Cool? That's it?"

"Yeah, it's cool. I like him. Even more, he's good to you..."

"There you go, always thinking of me..."

"Because you always think of me. I'd do anything for you, Mama."

Smiling, proud of the son I've raised, "I know you would, baby."

"Hey, something's smelling good in here," Reese's deep, rich voice fills the room as he enters, landing a big, wet smooch on my right cheek. "Good morning, Sean. Hope you're well this morning."

"I'm good, thank you. Are we still on for today?"

Still on for today?

"Wait, the two of you have something planned? And you didn't include me?"

"Oh, dear, not purposely. I'm just taking Sean out to a little fishing hole I've found since moving here last year. It's a guy thing...that's all," Reese tries to reassure me.

"Yeah, ok. Grab some plates, breakfast is ready," I roll my eyes, teasing them, cutting off the last eye on the stove.

———

With Reese and Sean out of the house, I can turn on my jazz music and relax in peace. After whipping up a mimosa, I kick off my black fur slippers and gently rest my shoulders and back against the arm of the couch. I close my eyes, deep in thought, then the doorbell rings.

"Good morning, Carissa. How you been?" the mailman, Greg, asks, handing over a box and stack of mail.

"I'm doing great, Greg. How's Martha?"

"She is good! About to retire in December. Our oldest is about to gift us with another grandchild. Can you believe it?"

Greg and I converse, sharing life stories for the next ten minutes before he runs along to finish his route for the day. I open the box to find the new shoes I purchased for Sean last week have arrived. He'll be happy to know that I got them after weeks of him throwing hints. I sit the box on the coffee table and sift through the other mail Greg left me with. At the bottom of the stack is a letter from the city council. The first paragraph entails an explanation as of why I hadn't received a notice. It appears something has been going on with the city council building downtown and they've relocated a few blocks over. The next meeting, which will include the hearing for the street name request, will be in four weeks. This is just about the best news I've had all day. Not able to focus on anything else, I work to gather all the documents I believe I'll need at the hearing. I want this street name change to go as smoothly as possible. Fortunately, my neighborhood is behind the movement so that alone should make things easier.

As I stuff the documents I have into a large white envelope for safekeeping, my phone rings.

"Hey, babe, are you busy?" Reese asks, his voice echoing.

"No, not busy. Am I on speaker?"

"Well, you're on Bluetooth...in my truck. I wanted to call and see if you'd be interested in going to dinner tonight. A new spot opened across town. I thought I could treat you and Sean since the two of you are always catering to me. What do you think? You down?"

"Am I...down? Oh, God, you've definitely been hanging around Sean too long," I snicker. "But, yes, I'm "down" for dinner. What time should I be ready?"

"In two hours," Sean blurts.

"Yes, two hours. I'll text you the location..." Reese states, ending the call.

———

My GPS leads me to a new soul food joint that my coworker mentioned to me some weeks back. As I pull into the parking lot, I see Reese and Sean waiting for me at the entrance.

We enter and the line's right at the door. I guess everyone in town has come out to try the new place. Within thirty minutes, we're seated in a booth; Sean on one side, Reese and I on the other. A waitress quickly comes over, welcoming us to the restaurant, and takes our drink order.

"So, did the two of you enjoy your outing?" I eye them both, curious as to what they've been up to.

"Yes..." Sean mutters, giggling after his comment.

"Yeah, ok. What are you two really up to?" I fold my arms over my chest, resting them on top of the table.

They eye one another, basically speaking with facial expressions. Now I'm suspicious but in a good way. What are these two up to?

The waitress comes back and takes our order. A large group of young adults, a mix of girls and boys, are seated at a large round table just across from us. They're a bit rowdy but I guess it's to be expected; they're young. After a short while, our food arrives, and the guys begin to share details about their outing.

"So, did either of you catch anything on this "fishing" expedition you've been on?" I question.

Reese leads, hesitantly stating, "Well, we didn't exactly go fishing..."

My brows raise, interest peaked.

"You're going to do it now?" Sean says, attempting to whisper.

Reese nods, shifting his body to the left toward me.

"Carissa, we've known one another for a few months now, but when I'm with you it feels like I've known you forever. I love the feeling that you give me; you make me feel new again. You make me feel whole..." Reese begins.

My bottom lip drops slightly, and my heart rate goes from zero to one hundred, as he takes my hands in his. Reese's lips are moving but I can't hear a word he's saying. I'm so nervous about what he'll say next.

Reese reaches into his pocket and pulls out a small white box, Zales embroidered in fancy gold lettering on the top of it. He pops the box open and there sits a small diamond ring, glistening under the light hanging over our table.

"Carissa, from this moment on, I want to make a dedication to you. I don't want to be in your life for just a season. I want to be here for a reason...a lifetime...if you'll allow it. I'm not here to rush things, as this isn't an engagement ring. This ring symbolizes my promise to you, to Sean, to be in your lives if you'd like to have me..." Reese recites, sweat beads forming around his hairline.

My heart melts at his proposal, especially after finding it's not an engagement ring. I'm not prepared for that step, I'm still working on my internal self. My eyes lock, staring into Reese's, grasping the words he's spoken are true, genuine. I look to Sean for confirmation and he smiles, mouthing, "I love you."

"I'm extremely blessed to have you in my life, Reese. It's as if the Lord put you in my path for a reason. I want to continue to get to know you, grow with you, be with you," I smile, allowing him to slide the ring on my right ring finger. I still wear my wedding ring on my left and I refuse to remove it until I marry again...if I marry again. Reese is aware and seems perfectly fine with it.

We continue with food, ordering a round of drinks, virgin for

Sean, to celebrate and wait for the waitress to come back to provide us with a dessert menu. Although we're in close proximity, communication between Reese, Sean, and I becomes more difficult by the minute. The group of young people that was seated next to us earlier has been a noise hazard. I look around at other patrons and they seem to be highly disturbed as well. The restaurant manager stops by, attempting to calm them for a second time. Instead, they become unrulier, some taking off, only leaving four people behind. Within minutes four dwindle to two.

"Do you see this," Reese mumbles, sipping the last bit of his cocktail.

"What's that?" I look up from my dessert.

"They're about to leave without paying..." he mutters, standing from the table.

I drop my fork and swallow the remainder of my food, watching attentively as Reese's tall, daunting stature moves toward the table across the way from us.

"What's going on with you young people today?"

"Excuse me?" one of the two girls left at the table replies to Reese, rolling her eyes.

Reese says something that Sean and I can't hear and then the unexpected happens.

"So, you're going to leave?" Reese spits, slamming his hands on the table.

His voice and the slamming are so loud that my body is startled, causing me to nearly spill my drink.

"Sir, I don't know what you're talking about. Wait, do you even work here?" the second girl stands, grabbing her purse.

"No, I don't work here, but I know exactly what you're trying to do here, and I won't stand for it..."

The girls laugh, gather their things, walk past Reese, headed toward the exit.

"See, it's folks like y 'all..." Reese shouts, a vein now bulging from the middle of his forehead.

The second girl turns to confront him, snapping, "Folks like y 'all? From the looks of it, you're part of the same population..."

"Nothing about us is the same. Nothing!"

"Ok, gramps! Come on Toya, let's get the hell outta here. Everyone's waiting on us," the second girl chuckles, brushing Reese's words off, turning away from him.

My mouth drops as Reese continues, bickering with the two young girls who have planned what I call a "dine and dash." It seems their plan was to simply eat and walk out with no intent on paying. I won't lie, it angers me that our young people still do this. There are better things to do than take and steal from your community.

"It's black folks like you; dumb, broke, living off the system. I bet twenty years from now, you'll still be doing the same shit you're doing here today. You'll be somewhere barefoot, pregnant, living in the projects on food stamps and Medicaid with fatherless children, blaming your troubles on the white man..." Reese rambles. "Always looking for a handout, a free ride, yet still want to blame it all on white supremacy. White supremacy my ass. All of you negros hold yourselves back! You're your own worst enemy!"

The words from Reese's mouth sting as they enter my ears. I look over and Sean and he's in total shock. I can bet anything he's thinking the same thing I am right now.

BAM!

I turn to see what the commotion is only to find that Reese has flipped over the table next to us where the young people were sitting and one of the chairs surrounding the table hit a small child in the back of the head.

"Reese!!!" I scream, standing to my feet.

He turns and looks at me much like a starving zombie would look at its next meal. His eyes are wide, his dark cheeks are flushed, and his fists are so tight that the veins in his hands are protruding; he's completely enraged.

His eyes leave me once again, and he's back to the same behavior; screaming and smashing things.

"Sean let's go. Right now!"

Stunned by all that's happened, Sean seems to be a bit hypnotized. I shove him, grab him by his hand, and drag him to the parking lot.

"Wait, what about Reese?" Sean stutters, nearly falling.

Everything that I want to say about Reese right now, I can't, not to Sean.

"Just get in the car!"

As I fumble through my purse for my keys, there's a tap on my driver's side window.

"Carissa, open up..." Reese pants, knuckles bloody.

"No!" I start the car.

"Mom, please. Just talk to him.... Please..."

The look in Sean's eyes is speaking volumes right now. He deeply cares for Reese.

Thinking of Sean, I let down my window.

"Yes?" I state firmly, looking forward and not at Reese.

"Please, let me explain..." he pants like a mad dog.

"What was that in there? You lost control...over nothing!"

"I know, I know. I didn't mean to. It's just, they were going to leave without paying...and..."

"And what? If they want to run out of a restaurant without paying, then let them! Let the restaurant deal with it!"

"I...I...I can't..."

"Yes, you can! You're not some damn superhero running around here. You're not the damn Hulk! I don't know who you are right now."

"Dammit Carissa!" he screams, cracking my window.

My eyes widen with fear. Never in my life have I had another human being get anywhere *near* physical with me and I won't start today. I throw my car into reverse, nearly backing over Reese, and floor it out of the parking lot.

"Mom are you ok?"

"I don't know, Sean. I don't know."

As we approach a red light just minutes from home, the phone rings.

"Tyson?" I answer, a bit shocked that he's called.

Tyson was Samara's first love, high school sweetheart, and college roommate. They were engaged before she passed. I always thought they'd make a great couple. I haven't heard from him since she passed, as he was so heartbroken afterward. I only talk to him in passing now.

"Mrs. Bennett, I hope you're doing well."

"I am, thank you. I hope you're doing fine as well. It's good to hear your voice..."

"Yours too, Mrs. C," Tyson clears his throat. "Look, I'm calling because I have some information for you that you'll want to hear."

"Ok...are you ok? Your parents?"

"Yes, ma'am, I'm fine. Much better now that this news just came across my desk."

Tyson started as an officer and over the years has been

promoted to detective on the local police department. He's one of the few African Americans they have.

"What news is that?" I ask, pulling into my garage, putting my car into park.

"I can't handle it directly, so a colleague came to me with it. It's about Samara. There's newly surfaced information regarding her case, big information. Please tell me you have time to come down to the station...like right now."

CHAPTER 7

4 Weeks Ago

"Detective Tyson Grant, please," I tell the receptionist with urgency.

She nods and immediately picks up her desk phone, dialing Tyson. He shows up in a matter of seconds, greeting Sean and me, escorting us to his office.

"You look good," I smile, hugging him.

"You do, too. And, Sean, man have you grown. It's good to see you, bro."

He and Sean shake hands and we each seat ourselves. As much as I want to catch up with Tyson, I want to know about Samara's case.

"So, what information do you have...about Samara," I pry, desperate for Tyson to speak.

He leans in, clasping his hands together on top of the desk, "Before her arrest, she recorded her encounter with the officer. The phone was omitted in the original case but thanks to the lawyer that you originally hired for the case, has been working behind the scene to get justice for Samara...for you guys."

Tears flow like the mighty Mississippi River, I've waited so long to hear something like this.

"Mrs. C, this is Detective Cross. He has been assigned Samara's case and can give you more details," Tyson smiles proudly, accompanying his colleague in to greet Sean and me.

"Mrs. Bennett, it's a pleasure to meet you. Your reputation proceeds you, and that of your daughter's as well. I am *truly* sorry for your loss, but I pray what I have to say today will bring you some comfort. Detective Grant and I have been working over the past few years, alongside your family law firm, to pull together information regarding your daughter's case. Each avenue that we've taken has been a dead-end, as much of the evidence that should have been handed over to us has been buried deep below the surface. But, today, with the help of your lawyer, we gained access to Samara's cell phone footage from the day of her arrest. The arresting officer's original testimony, his sole reason for arresting Samara, was that he felt threatened. That wasn't the case. We are to believe this footage was originally withheld by certain law officials to ensure those who were involved wouldn't be incriminated for their actions, along with other information that we've discovered during the time Samara was in jail..."

Goosebumps form and each fine strand of hair on my body comes to attention as Detective Cross delivers the news regarding Samara's case. There was so much information hidden when the trial regarding her death occurred. The system's supposed to be fair and justice. It was nothing near that for Samara or anyone else in similar situations over recent years.

"Ma, can I go to the vending machine? My throat is dry, I

need some water," Sean asks nervously, his left hand slightly shaky.

"Yeah, go ahead. Here are a few dollars for you," I respond, observant of his eyes and body language.

I know him too well. I can guarantee that he's leaving the room because it pains him to hear this about Samara. It was difficult enough to lose her four years ago. Talking about it here today just caused those feelings from four years ago, those exact feelings that I've been working so hard to suppress to move forward in life, are back. Internally, I'm an emotional wreck but I understand how necessary it is I stay focused at this point.

Sean exits, and Tyson closes the door behind him.

"Everything ok?" I frown at their strange behavior.

"Mrs. C, I'm somewhat glad Sean exited the room because I wasn't sure if you wanted him to see or hear this," Tyson starts, sitting next to me.

"Mrs. Bennett," Detective Cross starts, "We're not supposed to show you this information, so I beg of you please keep it hush. Detective Grant and I could get in a great amount of trouble..."

"No, my lips are sealed. I'm just grateful that each of you has been working on this to get Samara some justice."

Detective Cross hands over a document with a list of names; some are recognizable, and some aren't.

"What's this?"

"Two months prior to the release of Samara's cell phone and the footage within, we four individuals, all part of different police departments, come forward collaboratively with information on corrupt individuals working within their own stations. The names you see on that paper there are those that have participated in corrupt operations and are in the process of being taken down. This goes back as far as 11 years, so some are still on the force, and others have moved on. We are currently in the process of ensuring the whistleblowers are protected and that everyone named is implicated. This will cause each case they worked on or had a hand in to be reopened and reworked. Unfortunate to say, the Feds will most likely step in to assist as well."

"Wow!" I reply, shocked and utterly speechless with the list of names still in hand.

Tyson exits the room while Detective Cross and I continue to chat. He further explains the timeline for arrests of those who have been implicated and how I can move forward with Samara's case. We shake hands and I'm escorted out into the hallway, heading for the front lobby. I find that Sean and Tyson are talking.

"You boys catching up?"

"You could say that," Tyson replies. "Sean, it was good to see you. If it's ok with Mrs. C, take me up on that offer."

Sean nods, taking the car keys from me and walking out.

"Mrs. C, you good? Do you have any questions for us? Your lawyer will most likely contact you any moment now unless you reach out first."

"I want to say thank you for reaching out to me with this information. Since Samara left us, I've been struggling but Sean opened my eyes to what life should be. I've sought therapy and religious counsel, and my feelings have eased, but I've come to the realization that I will never be the same. The only thing I can do is accept life for what it is and make sure Sean lives a great one and stays out of trouble in the process."

"Yeah, I saw the news footage of you pulling him away from that riot. Good move, because not too long after a rifle was accidentally fired by a rookie officer. Fortunately, things were settled quickly, and the crowd disbursed shortly after. If I may be honest, I miss Samara beyond measure. I'm not the same since her passing. I thought that we'd spend the rest of our lives together. Things just came to a halt. My entire world ended that day you called me. It's been difficult to move forward. I try as best I can, but much of my time has been dedicated to obtaining justice for Samara. You know, if I had been able to do things a bit quicker she'd still be alive..."

"No, don't you dare blame this on yourself. There's no way we could have predicted the last time we'd see or speak with Samara. As much as I appreciate your dedication to Samara, I won't stand by and allow you to throw your life away. You're a great young man, you deserve happiness."

"This is why I've always loved you. You make things seem so...simple."

"Life isn't simple, but I've discovered ways to make mine less complicated. Why don't you come by the house sometime? I'm sure you could use the company, and, to be honest, Sean and I could as well. You're missed."

"Thank you. I'll take you up on that offer, soon I'm sure. If you have nothing else for me, I'll see you out."

I nod.

Tyson escorts me out of the lobby and into the parking lot where Sean is waiting in my SUV.

"Mrs. C have a good night..." he reaches for the handle of the driver's side door.

"Wait, Tyson, I do have a question for you."

"Yes, ma'am."

"Do you have contact information for a private investigator? I have some information I'd like to check out regarding Samara."

Tyson frowns but doesn't ask further questions. He reaches in his pocket for his phone, scrolls through his contacts, and provides me with a number to the top PI in the state. He says the police department uses this PI's services quite often.

He opens the door of my vehicle and helps me inside.

"The two of you have a goodnight. We'll speak soon."

I pull out onto the main street and get a glimpse of Sean's face.

"Sean, what's bothering you?"

"I'm fine, just tired. Today's been..."

"Rough, yeah, I know."

Though Sean says nothing is wrong, I know he's avoiding whatever the real issue may be. He and Reese have grown extremely close over the past months, therefore I'm sure today's events have left him just as confused as I.

4 Weeks Later – Present Day

Of all the days to get caught in traffic, today would be the day. I sit on the interstate and traffic is at a standstill. Over the past month, we've gotten rain has taken over, causing flash flooding statewide. Though it's not raining today, the main river has swollen and overflowed into certain portions of the city. You'd think that the locals would be used to seeing the high levels of water, but, no. As they ride by, they feel compelled to peek at the surrounding water. Someone's decision to look today seems to have caused a car accident which has delayed traffic.

For the next twenty minutes, I weave from lane to lane, slowly approaching my exit. I finally arrive at my destination, the designated meeting location for city council meetings. Already nearly a half-hour late, I risk parking in a handicapped spot, so I don't have far to walk. Taking on the folder with documents and my cell, I file in as quietly as possible and take a seat in the back-left corner of the room.

"Here's your agenda," my neighbor, Mr. Sandoval, whispers, handing over a double-sided printed document. It appears they've combined last quarters agenda with this quarter's, and the list of items for tonight's meeting is quite intensive.

According to Mr. Sandoval, they're on item three and my topic is item number twelve. We sit through some discussions that are, frankly, unnecessary, but I can't judge because when my matter comes forth, I want everyone's undivided attention.

"Next on the agenda, the proposal of a street name change made by Carissa Bennett," Councilmember Roy states, looking around the room, waiting for me to stand.

I stand and approach the podium, centered and facing the council directly. Mr. Roy takes a moment to inform the crowd of my request and mentions that necessary documentation was provided upon submission. Mr. Roy and the council allow those attending, the general public, to speak on the matter.

"I've lived in this neighborhood since I purchased my home at 27. I'm 78 now. I helped build this neighborhood with my own hands, and to watch it deprecate right before my eyes some years back hurt me deeply. Then along came Ms. Samara Bennett, a bright-eyed, head strong girl who brought a once broken neighborhood into a state of unity. Sadly, she was taken from us too soon. I don't know if my statement tonight will matter, but I'd hope each of you takes what I've stated into account. Without Ms. Samara Bennett, this neighborhood would still be in sham-bles. In her way, in a way that those in this neighborhood could understand, she cleaned these streets and brought peace again," Mrs. Mary Jones speaks, barely standing due to severe arthritis in her knees. She's a retired Air Force pilot and school teacher, and has a great standing in the community, with the state's political leaders, etc.

I mouth, "Thank you," as two gentlemen help seat her.

Two other individuals, whom Samara helped save their kids from entering the system, speak on my behalf, welcoming the name change.

"Sir, would you like to say something?" Mr. Roy inquires to a gentleman who's taken it upon himself to approach the podium and position himself next to me.

Giving me the side-eye, the gentleman clears his throat and proceeds to speak, stating, "I've been an active member of this community for most of my life. I was a Postmaster for 36 years and after retiring I took an active role in the neighborhood, being elected president of the Neighborhood Watch. I didn't know Ms. Bennett personally during her time here on this earth but from what I witnessed, she was nothing short of an aggressor..." Mr. Andrews expresses, shaking from head to toe.

I'm instantly angered.

"What do you mean she was "an aggressor," Mr. Andrews?"

"By aggressor, I mean she wasn't a rule follower. She always pressed issues, held protests, and so on. Those things weren't necessary, and quite frankly her actions led to the bickering and fighting we witnessed in the neighborhood on several occasions some years back. The police were called on many occasions. They were called enough to know her by name, knowing that if something happened that Ms. Bennett most likely had a hand in it," he expresses himself firmly, stepping closer to me, glaring down at me with his emerald green eyes.

"My daughter would never," my voice ascends, but his voice drowns me out as he directs his tone toward the council, "I don't believe that we should change the name of a street that's been in existence since the start of the neighborhood. It's Arrington Boulevard and that it should stay. Changing the name will only strike up controversy that we've long put behind us. This will cause people to move in from all over the place who don't need to be here. Let's move forward. I vote no for this change, and I hope others here tonight will stand beside me in my decision."

I stand still, flexing my hands, looking down at the podium that I've had to share with Mr. Andrews through his horrendous speech about my daughter and her agenda while here on this earth. The longer I stand next to him, the more my anger and frustration grow. I close my eyes, exhaling deeply, fully opening my hands so my palms are showing. Truthfully, I want to smack the hell out of this man for displaying this level of arrogance, ignorance, and lack of respect that he has tonight. In my fifty years here on this earth, I've seen some things, but never anything like this. To diminish or belittle the work that Samara put in, tiring herself in the process and choosing not to follow a path in her degree field, is below the belt. I pray it's not the case, but I believe his reaction to the name change request is simply because of Samara's melanin, her persistent activity, and advocacy for her brown-skinned brothers and sisters not only in the neighborhood but the thousands she reached through her life videos and podcasts. They're afraid to see a positive change for the minorities in the neighborhood, and I can guarantee that they want to keep the minority population at a minimum as they've been doing for years.

"I agree. This neighborhood has been established for years, and Arrington Boulevard was named after a prominent founding family in this very city many years ago. Why are we attempting to fix something that isn't broken?" another member of the neighborhood watch, Laci Stanton urges.

Two more individuals stand, protesting the street name change. Ironically, they don't even live in the neighborhood; they've simply decided to weigh against it. Typical.

"Of all things to fight over, this is not one. The street name won't devalue the street itself or the neighborhood, but instead, pay homage to a young woman who works diligently to revive it to its current state. Let's celebrate her victory, learn from her mistakes and defeats and continue to push this neighborhood and others in the right direction," I speak firmly, looking every soul in the building right in the eyes.

"Thank you, Ms. Bennett, for coming forth. Do you have any further information for us before we decide on the approval of your request?" Mr. Roy questions, appearing as if he's had enough for the evening.

"Only this..." I reply, handing over the documents I'd previously prepared to the council.

As I prepare to take my seat, "Councilman Roy, I have a comment." Roy nods.

"If you allow this street name change, I'll boycott every business here. I'll take my business elsewhere, somewhere that I'll be appreciated. That girl's reputation will run this into the ground. Next thing you know, these people will want to change every damn street name in the city!" a gentleman voices quite loudly, startling me.

"Just what in the hell do you mean by "these people," man? Who are you talking about?" a black gentleman stands, eyes glued on the other gentleman. I can see that comment has sparked something in him, as his jaw flinches uncontrollably.

"You know what he means!" a distant feminine voice speaks, staying hidden.

"You don't want no smoke!" the black gentleman speaks, stepping out into the aisle, not taking his eyes from the gentleman.

"Speak English!" the man barks.

My right shoulder is clipped, and I'm nearly pushed to the ground as three people rush past me. In what seems like slow motion, the entire room breaks into chaos putting the council on alert. Councilman Roy jumps over the table at which they're seated and attempts to stop the fights only to be shoved to the ground, being trampled by the mass.

Internally I panic, rotating 360 degrees, trying to find a way out of the madness.

"Come on, let's get you out of here," I hear a voice say, grabbing my hand from behind, pulling me through the crowd and out the entrance.

"Oh, Mr. Sandoval, thank you!

"Anytime. Listen, get out of here now and get home to Sean."

"Of course. Wait, are you not leaving?"

"Oh, definitely, I'm headed to my vehicle now. I can only imagine how this will turn out," he scoffs, holding my vehicle door open as I climb inside.

Unexpectedly, a gun fires three times from inside the building and all I hear are screams. Fearful, I drop my head and grip the steering wheel.

"Go! GO!" he slams my door, running off to his vehicle.

These city council meetings always have police standing by so I'm sure one of them has fired off inside the building to gain attention and cease fighting. Like a thief in the night, I ride away as quick as I can, praying no one has been harmed. All I wanted to do was pay tribute to my daughter in the city where she dedicated her life to helping others, and it's all gone down the drain due to folks who can't see past their own agendas, who can't accept change.

Overwhelmed, I pull into a gas station less than two miles from my house and let every bit of frustration and emotion flow from me. Crying and screaming all at once, I don't know what more I can do. I'm not any closer to getting Samara the positive recognition she deserves than I was the day she died.

Catching me off-guard, my phone rings.

"Hello?"

"Mrs. Carissa Bennett?"

"This is she. Who's speaking?"

"This is PI Jerome Flint. I'm done with my investigation. Would you like the results by phone? Or would you prefer I hand deliver and speak in person?"

I respire slowly, heart thumping a mile a minute.

"I'm nearly home. Can you come now?"

"I'm on my way."

CHAPTER 8

Samara Bennett's POV
4 Years Ago ~ Wednesday, July 29, 2015

"You do know you don't have to travel alone? Right?" Tyson gropes me from behind as I rinse the remaining dishes in the sink before placing them in the dishwasher.

"I know, but you have things to do as well. I'm fine to go alone. Really. I'll be staying with Stephanie while I'm there."

"I do not doubt that you'll be fine, I just don't want to let you out of my sight. You know I'd follow you anywhere..." Tyson whispers, lightly running the tip of his tongue over the rim of my ear. He knows that's my sweet spot.

"Oh, no sir. If you start something, we won't be able to stop. If I don't leave within the hour, I won't make it in time to meet Steph for dinner."

"Alright, alright. I'll let you go. But when you get back, it's on and poppin'."

"I wouldn't have it any other way," I kiss him, allowing him to pull me into his chest, engrossing me into his masculine grasp.

After a mini makeout session, I quickly gather my things and load them in the car, with Tyson's help.

"Call me when you make it?"

"I will..." I respond, positioning myself in the driver's seat.

"Samara..."

"I will call as *soon* as I make it. I promise."

"Ok," he closes the door.

I let the driver's side window down and smile at Tyson. We've practically been inseparable since we first met. It's as if we were destined to be together.

"Have a safe trip," he nods.

As I roll the window back up, he places his hand inside the car.

"Hey, I love you, Future Mrs. Grant."

"I love you, too, Mr. Grant," I smile proudly, giving him one last kiss for the road.

He stands in the driveway as I back out. As I pull off, I watch in my rearview and he stands roadside. I watch from the rearview until I can no longer see him.

———

I cross the Stateline and dial Steph to let her know I'll be at her place within an hour should traffic allow.

Ding

"Damn," I swear, hitting the steering wheel. I've got 15 miles to empty.

Two miles up, I pull into a station to fill up, grabbing a bag of skittles and a bottle of sweet tea. Back on the road, I have only 38 minutes to my destination.

———

"Take exit 192 in two miles," my GPS sounds off as I make it into city limits.

I take my exit and merge onto a residential street, only blocks away from Steph's apartment complex. My phone line trills through my car speakers; it's Stephanie.

"I'm almost there. Just a few blocks away..."

"Great! My parents came over. They want to see you before we head out to dinner tonight. I hope that's ok."

"Perfectly fine. I haven't seen them since we graduated college. Do you need anything before I arrive? I can make a pitstop."

"No, we can stop..." Stephanie begins, but a passing ambulance overshadows her voice.

I squint at the sound of the sirens, they make me nervous. I haven't been the same since my father died. Though it's been one year since his passing, I feel as if he just departed yesterday. His passing is still fresh, not just for me but for my mother and my baby brother Sean as well. The night he passed, I remember being awakened by sirens, paramedics filing the hallway of our quaint three-bedroom home. I vividly recall him being carried on a stretcher, limp and lifeless. Drowning in tears, I held my brothers' hand as paramedics loaded my father into the back of the ambulance. Though my mom was calling out to us, we stood curbside watching as the ambulance sirens echoed through the neighborhood. It's interesting how life plays out. I wasn't supposed to stay with my parents that night, Tyson and I were to travel out of state, but I'd contracted a stomach bug, so we put off our trip, staying at my parent's place for a couple of days. I never imagined I'd see my father pass firsthand, but I couldn't visualize not being near during such a time. My mother doesn't know, but I fell into a deep depression after my father's death. I found it hard to get up for work, so I quit. Soon after I found it hard just to get out of bed alone. I stopped caring for myself mentally, physically, emotionally, and spiritually. I was bad off, but Tyson never lost faith in me. He practically dragged me to the doctor; I was diagnosed with severe anxiety and depression. Oddly enough, my doctor prescribed me medicinal marijuana. It helps at the moment, but after it fades the memories, the thoughts, my anxiousness, my depressive thoughts resume. Over the last year, I've simply found myself existing, trying my best to make the most of life's moments with my mother, brother, and fiancé.

My hands become jittery, so I pull over to the nearest shoulder and take a breather.

"Lord, please be with me. Calm my nerves, Lord. As you know, I need this job. Tyson and I are struggling but are ready to create a new path, but with your guidance I know we'll be fine," I pray aloud.

I scramble through my purse for a pre-rolled joint, lighting it up quickly, taking it to my lips for a quick hit. I probably shouldn't be smoking it in the car, but my nerves are on edge, especially since that ambulance passed. A few hits calm me and I veer back onto the street. I take to the left-hand lane to pass two vehicles and then notice a police car in my rearview. I check my right mirror, clearing myself to get over so that I'm out of his path. As I merge, so does he. Damn, blue lights.

"What the hell did I do?" I wonder, pulling over on the right shoulder. The cars that I originally passed surpass me.

It takes a few minutes, but I watch in the left rearview mirror as the officer, Caucasian, lean, and handsome with a cocky stature, approaches my vehicle.

He taps on the driver-side window and I roll it down just enough for him to speak to me.

"Good evening, ma'am. Do you know why I pulled you over?"

"No, I don't. Why?" I snap, a bit irritated because I know I've done nothing wrong.

"You merged from the left lane to the right without signaling. Were you aware of that?"

"No, I wasn't aware. I was simply attempting to get out of your way, as I noticed you were catching up to me quickly."

"Well, you did. License and registration please?"

Without thinking, and using my peripheral vision to watch him, I quickly lean over toward the glove box to retrieve my registration.

"Ah, slowly...please..." he places his right hand on his holstered firearm, widening his stance.

I scoff sarcastically.

"Is there a need for you to place your hand on your gun? Do you feel threatened by me?"

Repositioning his stature, he exhales deeply, "Ma'am, license and registration please..."

I roll my eyes and continue to slowly reach in the glove box for my registration and then to my purse for my license. Unable to find it at first glance, I dump all my belongings out into the passenger seat to locate my wallet. I take my cell phone from the pile, lying it on my right thigh, and the officer repositions again, this time unbuckling his holster for easier access to his gun.

I want to, but I don't say a word. I simply hand over the information he's asked for so that he can leave my presence for a moment.

Once again, my phone line trills through my car speakers. It's my mom this time.

"Samara Brielle, why did your fiancé have to communicate with me your plans for this week? Were you not interested in explaining to your mother that you'd be traveling miles upon miles out of state by yourself? I knew you were looking for work out of state, I could have ridden along, kept you company," my mother, Carissa, shouts through my speakers.

"Mama, I needed to do this alone. You know Tyson and I are trying to find a new beginning. This is my way of doing that. His career allows him to move at leisure, mine doesn't. He already has a transfer approval in the event I find employment out here. You know I can't move without a job."

"And you know that I've offered to help you and Tyson countless times until you two are on your feet."

"Mom, we can't live off you. You've been struggling enough paying off dad's medical bills and taking care of Sean. We got this. We'll be fine and on our feet in no time. I promise. Just...let us handle this one. We need to do this for ourselves."

"Fine. I'll try. Anyway, where are you now?"

"I'm actually on the side of the road. I've been pulled over by the police for not signaling during a lane change. Typical. They have nothing to do down this way so stopping people for small, insignificant reasons has to do."

"POLICE? What? I will stay on the phone with you until you are safely on your way again."

Noticing the officers getting out of his vehicle, I reply, "No, no need to do that. I'll be fine. He's coming back now.

I'm sure I'll get a ticket. I'll call you when I've made it to Steph's."

"You're just like your father; stubborn. Please call me. Don't make me have to call you, Samara."

"Ok, I will."

"You better! And watch your mouth. I know how you feel about the police, especially with all that's happened recently. You tend to get a little sassy, so tone it down, ok?"

"Ok, Mama, I gotta go," I end the call, not saying bye or I love you. I love Mama, I do, but at times she can be a bit over-bearing. I know it's for the best but sometimes she's just relentless.

"Here are your license and registration back," he shoves my information back through the window, practically throwing it at me. "You do understand that being licensed to drive is a privilege and not a right, correct?"

"Excuse me?"

"A licensed driver would know not to improperly change lanes. You could have caused an accident...anything..."

"I understand your point, sir, but the vehicles I passed were several car lengths behind me. I'm sure no one would have been harmed. But thank you for explaining that..." I roll my eyes, putting my things back in my purse.

"Roll the window down..." he states firmly, placing his hand inside the vehicle.

"Excuse me? Why? I don't have to do that. This is my vehicle. What's next, you want to get in here and sit with me?" I follow up, a bit offended at his tone.

"I won't' ask again!" he growls.

"No, and with the tone, you're using, I'm feeling unsafe," I reach down for my phone, turning on the video.

I begin speaking into my phone while it records, explaining the officer's behavior since he stopped me and his request for me to let my window down all the way although I've expressed I feel uncomfortable.

Noticing he's highly perturbed by my actions, he snaps again, throwing the backside of his left fist against my window to break it.

"Oh, my God! What are you doing?"

"Let the damn window down. If I have to ask again...."

"What? Are you going to hurt me? Huh?"

"You know what, I was only going to give you a warning, but since you want to bitch about it, I'm writing you a ticket!" he slams his board onto the roof of my car.

"Fine, do what you must so I can get outta here," I continue, nearly done with putting my items back in my purse.

"Whoa, is that what I think it is?" he exclaims, looking at my purse.

I look over to see what he sees, and I see nothing.

"Step out of the car."

"What?"

"STEP OUT OF THE FUCKIN' CAR!"

He opens my door, leaning in over me to unbuckle my seatbelt. I push him away, feeling beyond uncomfortable. He's in my personal space and my anxiety is spiking by the second.

"Sir, please stop!"

"Get your ass out of this car!" he snarls, finally unbuckling my belt, tugging at my left arm.

"NO!" I pull back, leaning on the center console.

"If you don't get out, I'm going to light yo' ass up with this taser. Your choice! You've got three seconds! One...two...thr..."

I begin screaming, yelling into the video on my cell phone. At this point, I fear for my life. This man could seriously hurt me, and I have no clue why. Why is he being so aggressive with me?

My mother's voice echoes in my mind.

"You tend to get a little sassy, so tone it down, ok?"

I stop struggling and comply, but it's too late.

SMACK!

He knocks me right across the face, knocking the breath out of me. Something inside me sparks, my adrenaline kicks in, and I punch him back with my right hand. He takes my left leg, pulling it out of the car.

"Stop!" I cry out, trying to get out of the car before he completely drags me out onto the ground.

Once out, he immediately locks my arms behind my back, throwing me over the trunk of my white Kia Elantra.

"Got dammit, you made me do this," he screams, out of breath. He seems just as panicked as I.

From his radio, he calls for backup.

"Why are you arresting me? I didn't do a thing but tell you that I didn't want to roll my window down," I shout in pain from the grip he has on my arms.

"I saw the contraband in your front seat! I'm taking your ass to jail."

Before speaking, I think long and hard about the "contraband" that he could have seen in my car. I don't do drugs. What is he referring to? And then it dawns on me! The joints! I rolled them a couple of days back to prepare for this trip. I figured I'd need something to calm my nerves in preparation for my interview tomorrow.

"Wait, there's a misunderstanding. What you saw in my front seat isn't illegal; it's medicinal. I have a medical marijuana card.

"Yeah, right. Typical of you to say that knowing that I've seen it. I'm taking your ass in. You can explain it to the judge."

The trunk of my car is steaming hot, so I attempt to keep my skin from making contact. When I raise my head up for the third time to keep my face from melting against the car, he shoves my head down, holding it there. I wiggle but to no avail.

"You just won't stop! I can show you better than I can tell you."

He pulls me from the trunk to the roadside in the dirt. He forces my petite, 123 lb. body to the ground, face down, sinking his knee into my back.

"Oh, you're hurting me. You're hurting *me*," I begin to sob from the pain. If he presses any harder, I feel as if he'll break something...my back.

Once again, he forces my head down, this time into the dirt, as he climbs on top of me. He straddles my backside as he smothers my face into the dirt. I begin to choke, as I've inhaled it through my mouth and nostrils. He slaps the cuffs on and laughs, stating, "Now, we're going to wait right here until my backup arrives. She should be here any moment.

For the next seven minutes, I lay face down in the dirt, feeling as if my arms are going to separate from their sockets and my wrists are going to snap. His help arrives timely and I beg and plead with her to help me, that it's been a misunderstanding regarding my arrest. She doesn't listen either, she sides with him. They throw me into the back of the patrol car and they both proceed to search my vehicle, tearing it apart, throwing my belongings in every direction.

Detained and in the back of the patrol car, we ride by my

vehicle and I realize my phone is in there. I can't contact anyone to let them know of what's happened. If my last few years as an activist have taught me anything, it's that I have the right to a phone call. I'll use that to call either my Mom or Tyson to find a lawyer and get me out of this mess.

CHAPTER 9

Samara's POV cont

"**O**UT!" the officer shouts, pulling me out of the backseat of the patrol vehicle onto my feet. I didn't realize until now, the backseat is very cramped. I nearly fall to my knees climbing out.

As I'm brought into the station, I gain a glimpse of myself in a mirror. Dirt is embedded around the perimeter of my locs, my eyes, nose, mouth, and neck. I'm ashamed to even mention the condition of my clothes. I appear and feel filthy.

"Gibson, you're back with one I see," a shorter, stout, middle-aged officer jokes.

"Well, you know, I do what I can. Gotta protect and serve, right?" Officer Gibson snickers, smirking.

Such an asshole! It burns me alive to hold my tongue, there's so much I could say right now. But I must remain silent, watchful, and pray. After all, this is what I teach those in my community when in situations such as this. If the recent deaths of my

African American people have taught me anything, it's to comply to the best of my ability. Though, it has become quite common for compliance to be a right of way to bring harm to or kill Black people. Either way, we lose and loved ones are left to mourn their dead. Therefore, I take pride in my work, why I give my last to those who need it, why I get out of bed and post up at the police station; to provide protection and service to *my* people.

"I'm going to remove the cuffs, if you do anything stupid you will regret it. I will make your time here a living hell. If you don't believe it, try me," Officer Gibson whispers in my left ear, leaving an eerie feeling in my gut. Aside from how he's treated me, there's something about this man. I can feel a presence from within him; a dark one, an evil one.

Rather than saying something I might regret, I remain silent, only nodding my head.

My fingerprints are taken, and I'm stripped and searched by a female guard, forced to shower, and given an orange top and bottom along with a set of slippers and socks. How welcoming.

As I'm escorted to my cell, I pass several cells, all with at least two people in them; mostly men. I only see one female and she looks to be high, probably on meth from the looks of her teeth and skin. I see no empty cells that I could be placed in and I pray they don't place me with that lady. On second thought, it doesn't matter where they place me. I'll be out of here soon. I'm escorted around a corner to a cell that's near the back entrance of the jail. There's enough room for at least four people but the room's empty.

"Step inside," Officer Fatass, well the guy that cracked a joke with Officer Gibson, pushes me. Nearly losing my footing, I'm thrown inside the cell. He has me turn around and stick my hands out through a feeding hole in the door so that my hand-cuffs can be removed.

"Settle in, it'll be a long night," he chuckles, walking away.

I quickly look around, noticing the condition of the cell I'm in. The paint is peeling from the blocked cement walls, the concrete floor appears as if it hasn't been swept in weeks, the shower looks like it holds a host of diseases, and there is not a mat, blanket, pillow...nothing.

"Hey, I don't have anything to rest on!" I bang on the door.

"Rest on that ego of yours. Officer Gibson told me how feisty you were out there. I see you've piped down now that you've been brought into the station. Jail changes things. Maybe it'll help tame your inner Africa..." he bursts into laughter, walking away.

"Fuckin' pig!" I slur, banging on the door again.

Just how in the hell am I supposed to get comfortable in here? Thank God I won't be here long.

The cell door flies open. Uh oh, Officer Fatass is back.

"What did you call me?" he glares, breathing vigorously.

"You heard me," I roll my eyes, looking away, walking toward the metal slab that I may have to call home tonight.

He roughs me up, throwing me against the wall by the trash can.

"Oh, I'm a pig huh?" he holds his robust, stubby fingers around my throat.

"Did I stutter?"

SMACK!

He takes his hand right across my face. It doesn't faze me. Out of retaliation, I spit...right in his face.

"You fuckin' bitch! You black bitch!"

"Whoa, whoa, hey, what's happening in here?" the female officer that helped Gibson runs in shouting.

"She spit on me!! Fuckin' cunt!" Fatass wipes away the spit angrily.

"You know you can't put your hands on this woman. Get the hell outta here. You're not supposed to be in here with her alone anyway! Are you trying to lose your job? You know you have a family at home to care for!"

She talks Fatass down and he leaves.

"Thank you," I respond, trying to catch my breath.

"Don't thank me yet..."

"What do you mean?"

"Hmm, nothing. Settle in."

"What about my phone call? I need to call my family! I have people looking for me! They must be worried."

"You just lost your phone privileges. With a better attitude, maybe you'll get your call tomorrow morning."

She slams the door behind her.

Thursday, July 30, 2015

I wake to the smell of metal and piss. God, I'm still here.

"Ah, you're awake."

"May I get my phone call now? You can't stall on giving me my call, I know my rights!"

"Pipe down, you'll get your call right after breakfast. Hope you like cold grits and sausage links," Officer Gibson sneers, closing the small opening in the door. I can hear his footsteps recede.

I close my eyes to pray, but my empty stomach interrupts. I didn't have a chance to get dinner last night. Matter of fact, they didn't offer me a thing here; only water. Someone eventually brought a mat, which was flat as hell, and a thin white blanket. I shivered all night.

Breakfast comes, and I choke down what I'm given, though it tastes horrid.

"Still here, I see..." Officer Fatass smiles from the opening of the door. He brings the lady cop along with him.

"Time for that phone call you begged for. Come on, out..." she cuffs me, escorting me down the hall toward the other cells that I'd originally walked past on my way in yesterday evening.

To my surprise, all cells are empty but two. The female has still locked away and there's a young man, who looks no more than twenty, in a cell as well. He looks frightened. I wish I could help him. If I were home, I *could* help him.

———

I dial my mother's number, calling collect.

"Samara! Samara? Where are you?" she bellows, not allowing me to say a word.

"I'm in jail, Mama."

"JAIL?"

I give my mother a full rundown of what happened during the traffic stop and my arrest, further explaining that the officer found my medicinal marijuana. I relay to her what I've been told by the female cop, that I won't be able to see a judge until Monday morning and they won't allow bail in the meantime. I also explain they stated they didn't see my medicinal marijuana card in the vehicle, though I know for sure I always keep it in my wallet.

"Don't you worry! I'm calling our lawyer right now! We have

been worried out of our minds. Steph has driven herself mad when you didn't show or answer your phone. We didn't know what to do. Tyson and I were just in the process of speaking with the police about a missing person report. Don't you worry, we're coming down and we're getting you out of this mess! Damn waiting until Monday. We will have you out of there *way* before then, ok?"

"Ok," I reply, becoming discouraged.

"Keep your head up. You're built for this. You help people in situations like this all the time, making sure that justice is properly served. You just hold on. We're on our way. If you can, call me. I will pick it up right away! Got it?"

"I got it. I love you, Mama. Please tell Tyson and Sean I love them as well."

"Will do. I love you, too, baby. I'll see you soon."

———

"Dinnertime!" the female guard bangs on the door as another person delivers the meal through the hole in the door.

I can honestly say I've never been so desperate for a meal. I haven't consumed anything since breakfast. Thinking of it now, I don't recall having any water today.

As I grab my tray, in steps my arch-nemesis.

"Eat up. We know you're deprived. For that we're sorry. Look, we even put you a little treat on there. Do you see it?" he smiles, revealing his grungy, yellow teeth.

I look down at the tray and notice a brownie. I manage to muster up a dry "thank you" so that I can be left to eat in peace. I tear into my food like it's the last supper, downing the 8 oz bottle of water they've given me, as they stand and watch me eat. It's ok. I'm fine with an audience.

"You know, Ms. Bennett, I did some homework on you. See, I know I'd seen you somewhere, and I have. My son was watching you on Facebook one day. It was one of those little videos that you do, talking to folks, hyping them up, leading them to believe change is among us."

"You mean my live videos? I'm glad your son was listening. He should be. Everyone should know of the injustices black communities face around this country."

"Injustice? I see no injustice. They go to jail, before the judge or jury, and they are tried. Whatever the result, they deserve it. Who are you to say that our justice system isn't fair? What do you know?"

"I know much more than you credit me for. Just like I know that neither of you should be in here right now," I roll my eyes, gulping down the last of my brownie.

"Don't get sassy with us!" Fatass snaps, standing from his seat.

"Whoa, not tonight Tolbert. She's feisty, I know. Just stand down."

I laugh at their behavior.

"Something funny?

"Yeah, you two. You're supposed to protect and serve your people, but all you do is sit and mock me, my cause in my community, and my Black brothers and sisters. I've used money out of my pocket to protect and help families in my neighborhood, white or black, who were in situations such as this. What have you done? Get up and put that funky ass uniform on every day? Does that make you feel better? Does that help you sleep better at night?"

Fatass stands, walks toward me, grabbing my chin in the palm of his sweaty hand, "Do you know what helps me sleep at night? Huh?"

"What?" I answer with attitude.

"Putting bitches like you behind bars."

"I didn't do anything wrong. All I did was change lanes without signaling and here I am, being treated like an animal. You treat animals better than you treat us. Our lives mean nothing to you. Typical though, especially for you cops in these podunk ass towns."

"You are an animal. A filthy...disgusting...animal..." he smears his private area in my face.

"Put that thing in my face again and I'll bite it off!" I growl, moving my face away.

He does it again and I react as I promised. I bite him in the seat of his pants. He's immediately angered.

"You bitch! You wanna bite? Oh, I got something for you to bite!" he unbuckles his trousers, allowing his small shriveled-up dick to pop out.

He slaps it in my face. I fight back as hard as I can because I know that he's only going to attempt to place it elsewhere next.

"Stop! Not now!" Gibson snarls.

"But...but..." Fatass stutters.

"NOT...NOW!"

Fatass releases his grip on me, throwing my head back against the cemented walls. They each collect themselves and walk away, closing my cell door behind them.

I let out a huge sigh of relief! Lord, send help! Please!

———

Saturday, July 31, 2015
12:01 AM

I wake to the sound of keys jiggling in the cell door. I open my eyes to find Fatass standing in the walkway.

Damn! When did I fall asleep? I wasn't even tired, considering I had already taken a nap. What happened? It's as if I've lost hours.

"How are you feeling? Feeling a little...high?"

I squint from the light shining in from the hallway.

"What? High?"

"You know how it feels to be high. Don't act fresh with me. I saw the contraband that was confiscated from your vehicle after your arrest."

"It's not recreational, it's for medicinal use only. I was diagnosed with severe anxiety and depression," I pant, trying to catch my breath.

I'm determined to sit up but my body just won't cooperate. It's like I'm somewhat paralyzed.

"I see those brownies did you good. Tasted good, didn't they?"

"The brownies? Oh, no! You laced the brownies!" I panic, fumbling over my words.

"Yeaaahh, that's right. You feel good, don't you? See, I knew everyone from the day shift would be gone by now and that I'd be back to see you, so I left a little surprise inside. You like it?"

"No...go...away. Get...away...from...me. I haven't...done... anything to you..." I answer, barely conscious. I can now tell that I've been drugged.

"You know, I sat and listened to some of your videos and podcasts. I'm impressed. You're a smart little cookie, aren't you?

Ha, you weren't smart enough, you landed yourself here. What would your supporters, all the boys, and girls you've helped, think of you now?"

"They'll still love me, support me even more than they do now."

"You think you a martyr? You ain't shit. Your name will die with you," he hisses, and for the first time, I hear his deep, southern accent. It's engraved in my brain, irritating my soul, my very being.

The look in his eyes displays wickedness to an extent I've never seen. His crystal blue eyes tell his story without him muttering a word; he's a bad man. From the looks of it, he wants to hurt me, he just hasn't figured out how to do it.

"I'm more than you will ever be!" I stand, stumbling, landing on the edge of the metal bed I've been resting on.

"Fight all you want, but you can't fight the contents of that brownie you consumed. Soon, you'll know your place; right under me. You know, I've never been this close to a black woman before..." he grins, walking toward me.

Bent over the bed, holding on as best I can, high out of my mind, I watch from my right-side vision as his black, worn-out tennis shoes approach me. He stops, towering over me, laughing cynically.

"Stand up and bend on the bed, face down."

"I wouldn't dare," I mumble, trying like hell to stay conscious.

"Oh, but you will..." he wraps his right arm under me, to lift me, but I exert what may be my last bit of energy. Using my left hand, I pull a loose metal piece from beneath the bed. I swing it out and upward, slicing through the right side of his neck.

Blood streams from his neck down onto his uniform. He clasps his hand on the affected area, screaming in pain.

"You black bitch!" he screams, slapping me against the bed.

In runs Officer Gibson.

"What's this?" he exclaims, watching as Officer Fatass loses more and more blood by the second.

Fatass quickly thinks of a lie, telling Gibson I attacked him, knowing well he was about to rape me, beat me, or worse.

"Back to your old ways, are we? I thought you learned your lesson during the arrest, but I see you're just like those thugs that follow you. Sad for you ..."

"You can kiss my black ass..."

"I wouldn't use the President's dick on a ten-inch pole! A white man of my caliber would never touch a heathen such as yourself. Besides, you're only good for one thing..."

He grabs me by the back of my neck, pulling me up on the bed. Another cop, a bit older, strolls in and pushes the cell door forward but not closed. Incoherently, I bear witness to them wrapping their nightsticks, prepping them for God knows what.

"Beat her..." Fatass growls, with the looking of death in his eyes.

Circling me, Gibson, Fatass, and the older cop begin beating me with their padded nightsticks. With each blow, I holler at the top of my lungs, balling in a fetal position to ease the pain. They don't let up, each blow is harder, more painful, than the next. Then, they stop. I make a break for it, scrambling for my feet, running to the door but my moment of escape is short-lived; the door's slammed in my face. Another cop enters, only standing at the door keeping watch. They resume, beating me relentlessly, until I can no longer move on my own.

Working together, the three cops place me into a chair that was positioned in the corner of the room when I first arrived.

"She's barely moving. Did we kill her?"

"Don't let me hear the word "kill" slip through your lips anymore tonight. We didn't do anything that no one else in our shoes wouldn't have done. Let's finish this so I can get home to my wife. I should have been home over two hours ago."

"And what will we tell Sarge when he makes it in?"

"We'll tell him..." Officer Gibson begins, coming up with a full, well-thought-out story regarding my arrest to the near death beating they just delivered. It's as if they've done this before as if they knew this was their plan for me all along.

"Look in the bottom of the trash can and get some spare trash bags. I know housekeeping leaves spare bags in the bottom," the older officer snaps at Officer Fatass, holding his neck. "Gloves...genius!" he snaps again.

The young officer left to guard the door runs to get gloves. They place them on and tie the bags together, making them look like a noose. Positioning it over my head, they sit me up straight and slip it over my neck as I sit in the chair lifelessly.

They tighten the noose so that it's snug, I can barely breathe. They file out one by one, only leaving the younger officer at the door to watch as I die. That's their words. He does as he's told.

Minutes pass but it feels like hours. Each waking second, I can feel myself slipping, my body becoming weaker, my eyesight fading. Then, from nowhere, there's a bright light. I peer to the right, finding a black gentleman in uniform standing in the doorway to my cell. He walks in slowly, examining my cell, the items covering the floor from my scuffle with those scumbags who call themselves policeman, protector of citizens, keepers of the law. He steps in front of me, examining. As he does, I examine him. He stands tall with deep, rich, chocolate skin and brown eyes.

I reach my bound hands out to him, struggling to reach his, crying out, "I'm so happy to see you."

My words are nothing but true. Since I arrived, this man is the only *black* person that I've laid eyes on. My heart rate increases, and I feel one last boost of energy, as I know I'm saved. Someone is here to help me. My brother, from another mother, is here to save me.

"Help...me...please..." I let out a labored breath.

He leans in and chuckles, "Oh, now you want help? Where was your willingness to comply, to beg, when you were on the side of the highway? Huh? Where was your willingness to comply and beg for mercy when you hurt my fellow officer?"

"Wait, what? I didn't do...anything," I gasp for a breath, scraping my brain to comprehend exactly what he means.

"It's niggas like you that give the rest of us a bad name. It's your fault you're in here, that you're in this condition. And you want to play the victim? Ha, now that's a joke for the books. Now, we can't let you leave. And, of course, I'm the one that must help clean up this mess that Doughboy made. Hmmm, what to do with you?" he circles me.

"Please, I just want to go home..."

"Oh, but you can't. After all, that's occurred here, you think we'll just let you go home?" he levels with me, allowing his hot breath to burn my eyeballs.

"From one black person to another, help me. If I were in your shoes and you were in mine, I'd help you..." I cough, noose tightening.

"See, that's the thing pretty girl, I'm not in your shoes, am I?" As he leans in closer, I get a close look at his name.

"Officer Thompson, is it? You can kill me here tonight, but my name *will* live on. They may not catch you now, next year, or the year after, but they will catch you. Everything that you've done to harm another innocent being will come back to haunt you ten-fold."

"Not tonight..." he smirks, using a towel to cover his hand, pulling the noose tighter.

I kick, scrambling, trying to catch my next breath, but it doesn't help. I gurgle spit, fighting tirelessly to hold on to my life. As my eyesight fades to blackness, I look over to the guard, mumbling, "Don't let me die in vain. Tell...my...truth..."

My body relaxes, and my last breath slips from my from within.

CHAPTER 10

Present Day

"Sista Bennett, please come in. It's good to see you," Pastor Henry gestures for me to sit.

"Thank you for meeting with me on such short notice. I know you're a busy man."

"I'm never too busy to meet with any of you. You are God's people, my people. I'm here at his service."

"I'm glad to hear that because I need the Lord now more than I ever have."

Intrigued, Pastor Henry leans in, taking my hands in his, "What's going on Sista Bennett? How can I be of help?"

"I recently discovered some information regarding Samara's death that has rocked me to my core. For the last four years, I've prayed for an answer, for absolution, and now that it's near, it's like I'm afraid of it. Why do I feel this way?"

"This is quite normal. You know, we tend to pray to the Lord for things, for answers to unanswered questions, but sometimes when we get what it is, we've asked for we don't necessarily know how to receive it...comprehend it. That make sense?"

"Yes, it does," a teardrop falls from my right eye.

"What you do now is pray to God for the strength you need to accept the answer he has given you. Now, you said this had something to do with Samara? If it's okay, do you mind if I ask what it is? You know she was like a daughter to me."

"Yes, she was. Always begging to follow behind you and the first lady. She claimed she was treated like a queen when she was at your place."

"She was. First Lady and I couldn't have children so First Lady was sure to treat Samara as if she was a daughter. She *was* our daughter, just from another mother. I thanked God every day for bringing you and your family into my church, for bringing Samara into our lives. It took my wife many years to get over not being able to conceive, Samara helped fixed that."

"It's good to hear Samara had such a positive influence on the two of you as well. New evidence has surfaced, regarding Samara's arrest and death. Some officers have come forth to bear witness to what happened to Samara during her time in that hellhole of jail that she died in."

Pastor Henry's jaws drop, tears streaming from his eyes. "I'm grateful to hear this, but also sadden as only the Lord knows what Samara endured during her time there. Sista Bennett, you've worked so long, so hard, to seek resolution for her death, but I must say something. Do not allow the wrongdoing of others to poison you, to shadow the light that lives in you. Ephesians 4:31-32 states, *Get rid of all bitterness, rage, and anger, brawling and slander, along with every form of malice. Be kind to one another, tender-headed, forgiving one another, as God in Christ forgave you*. Allow God to live and work through you, be a vessel, and all will work out in your favor."

"Thank you, Pastor."

"You are most welcome. Please, send my best to Sean. And, remember, I'm here for you always."

———

Finishing up dinner, I set the table and turn on some light jazz music to set the mood.

"What's with the music," Sean scrolls in, smelling like the outdoors.

"Uh, firstly, you know I like jazz. Secondly, go wash up for dinner. Reese will be here any minute."

"You know, I think I'll skip dinner tonight," Sean mutters, turning his back to me.

"What's going on with you?"

"Nothing."

"Sean, yes, it is. Tell Mom what's going on. Please?" I grab his right shoulder.

He snatches away, hitting my hand.

"Now just what in the hell's gotten into you? Since when do you hit your mother?"

"I didn't mean to hit you, I'm just upset right now and would like it if I could be alone."

"I see. I've been allowing you to hang with Eric a little too much lately. Is that what the problem is? I told you, Sean, that boy is nothing but trouble. You're better than this!"

"Ma, stop! It's not Eric. It's not him, it's everything that you're blind to! I just...I can't..." he stomps away.

I run after him, but the doorbell sounds.

"You're early," I greet Reese at the door.

"And you look stunning," he grins, kissing me on my left cheek.

Reese walks straight for the kitchen, washing up for dinner, seating himself at the dining table.

"It's quiet. Where's Sean? Out with Eric?"

"He's in his room," I sniffle.

Reese stands, approaching me, "Have you been crying?"

"No, just my sinuses."

"Are you sure? We can sit and talk if need be."

"I'm sure."

"Well, sit with me anyway. I want to speak with you for a moment before dinner starts."

I frown a bit but seat myself as he's asked.

"What's going on?"

"Well, today officially makes one year that we met on that elevator. I remember it like it was yesterday. I'd been through so much, some of which I've managed to blackout, and you were a ray of sunshine that walked in and brightened my dark days. For that, I thank you...and God..."

I stare in amazement at Reese's words. The look in his eyes expresses his genuineness.

Interrupting us, "Sean, there you are! I've been texting you like crazy, trying to see if you wanted to check out a new place that I'd found. Your mother told me that you started playing a new sport and your coaches have been keeping you quite busy."

"Yeah, you could say that," Sean reacts sluggishly.

"Come, come sit with us," Reese gestures.

Sean plops down in a seat across the table from us. We all grab hands and pray, and then I break out the food.

"This dinner is amazing!"

"You always say that," Sean groans, chomping on his baked chicken.

"Sean, what? What is wrong with you?" I whisper, a bit ashamed of his behavior.

"I told you, I'm good."

"Young man, you can't talk to your mother like that," Reese demands, dropping his fork.

Sean slams his hands down on the table, looking directly at Reese, and says, "You are not my father. You will *not* tell me what I can and cannot do...what I can and cannot say. You have *no* right."

"Sean Anthony! Out of my presence, and to your room, now!"

"Gladly!" he kicks his chair back, letting it fall back to the floor.

"What's going on? I know I haven't been here in a while but so much has changed," Reese stands, walking after Sean.

"Reese, don't. Let him be."

"You're right. He's right; I'm not his father. And I have no right to act as such," he looks around the living room, confused.

I just stand and stare, in awe. Just when I think I have things figured out, life throws another curveball.

"Well, I'm not hungry anymore. Wine?"

Reese nods in agreement.

We're over an hour and four bottles of wine into conversing, and Sean's yet to come out of his room.

"Did you redecorate," Reese stands, wandering around the room looking at photos that I've recently decided to place in my living room?

"No, just brought out some photos that I never should have taken down," I reply, standing with him.

"Who's this beautiful soul?"

"That's my daughter, that's Samara."

"So, this is the beautiful Samara?" he takes her college graduation picture from the mantle.

"Yep, that's my baby."

"You must miss her dearly," he turns to smile at me, placing the picture back in its place.

"Hmm, funny you say that," I reply, stepping closer to him. "I do miss her, more than anyone could ever imagine. She was taken far beyond her time."

"Did you hit a breakthrough with your therapist? The pictures weren't out before, but they are now."

"I did, and with God. I finally learned to do and accept things in my way...on my own time. I'm learning that things come full circle."

"Yeah, I'm ashamed to say, but I only learned that a couple of years ago. Like you, I've gone through some things that I've had to learn and grow from. I'm not proud of the person, the husband I once was, but I'm a better man from it all. I follow God now, thanks to you."

"Thanks to me?" I snicker.

"Yeah, thanks to you and Sean, I'm a better me. Why'd you laugh?"

"Let's sit and chat, shall we?" I turn off the jazz music, leaving us to silence.

"What's going on? You look bothered. Talk to me."

"You know, we never really talked about your time in the military and police force. Did you like it? I ask because Sean had once expressed some interest in being a Marine. Like his mother, my first mind tells me no. I don't want him to put his life in danger that way, but then I realized that there are so many dangers right here at home. I can try to protect him from them all, but I can't."

"That's true. We can't protect the children from everything and everyone."

"So, did you ever deal with young girls or boys coming into your presence, needing your guidance and expertise?"

"On several occasions, but not all of them deserved the help."

"Not all of them? How did you determine that? How did you determine who deserved help and who didn't?"

"It's all in the attitude, the demeanor. Many of the kids I ran into were in bad living situations and a product of it. No matter how many times they entered the system, no amount of talking or guidance would be enough?"

"Hmm, I see. So where did you work? I know you only moved here within the last two years or less."

"I worked for some time in Georgia, then Texas. After that, I decided to retire and took a much-needed sabbatical."

"Yeah, we all need that at times," I stand to my feet once again, walking toward the computer desk to grab something.

Reese gives me a weird look but continues to down his wine.

"July 29, 2015. Does that ring a bell to you?" I ask, sitting in the chair positioned at the desk.

"July 2015...no, should it?" he sits the wine glass down, scooting forward on the couch.

"Maybe," I shake my head, looking down at the papers in my hand.

"What about the name...Samara Brielle Bennett? That ring a bell for you at all?"

"Other than the fact that it's your daughter's name, no. Hey, babe, what's going on? Am I supposed to know the answer to these questions? Why are you asking me this?"

"You should, but for one reason or another you don't."

"Carissa, honey, please tell me what's going on. You're scaring me. Why are you about to cry?" he rushes over to me. I put my hand up, blocking him from coming any closer.

He frowns, still confused.

"I'll break it down for you. On July 29, 2015, my daughter, Samara Bennett, the young lady you see on the picture there, was arrested for not letting her car window down. An officer and his larger-than-life ego landed her behind bars in a small, redneck jail."

"Ok. I still don't understand why you're telling me this."

"I'm telling you this because new evidence has come to light in my daughters' case, although she was killed just over four years ago. The footage from her cellphone, after being held purposely, has been released, along with another video taken by a young rookie officer during the time of her death."

"Oh, wow! What can I do to help? I can call some of my old buddies and get you anything you need. Just say the word and I'll get on the phone now."

I burst into laughter, "You don't get it do you?"

"Get what, Carissa? Talk to me!" he snaps, coming closer. I raise my hand to him again.

"I hired a private investigator to look into the officers that were initially named to be part of Samara's death. I found some very interesting information. You want to know what else I found?"

"Go ahead. I know you're going to tell me anyway."

"You're right, I am. I found *your* damn name in the mix.

YOUR NAME, Reese! What, did you get close to me in hopes that I wouldn't find out? Is this all a game to you?"

"Me? What?"

"Reese, cut the crap, stop the act! My private investigator was so good, he found out that you've been institutionalized for quite some time following the death of my daughter. He found that you'd only recently gotten out right before you met me. I find it funny that after all the time we spent together, that you spent with my son, not one time did you mention that or the fact that you were seeing a therapist. You know, I not once asked myself where you were coming from when I met you that day on the elevator. I just assumed you were part of my prayers. Now I know you did come into my life as part of my prayers to the Lord. He brought you into my life, so I could meet you for myself, see the man you are for myself. It all makes sense now, why you didn't know Samara, Sean, or I; her story, her work in the community. I mean, Samara's story made national news. Her face was everywhere, so was mine. You went to therapy and blocked it all out. You blocked it all out and tried to move on like it never happened; you tried to make a new life for yourself."

Reese doesn't say a word, he only closes his eyes, breathing in and out slowly, rapidly shaking his leg. Without notice, he springs to his feet then drops to his knees.

"Carissa, sweetie..." he cries out, eyes glazed over. "That exact moment has haunted me for years. Day after day, I could see that young woman's face, among others, in random places, in my dreams. Of all my wrongs, this one hurt the most, it cut the deepest."

I don't say anything, I only fumble around with the DVD player to play the video of the officer who recorded what happened to Samara up to her last breath. I press play and it starts. I watch Reese's face as he looks on at what his fellow officers, his boys in blue, did to my daughter.

"She cried out to you for help!" I grit, trying to keep my composure with Sean a couple of rooms down.

"I...I was in a bad place in my life then. I became lost internally, looking for ways to deal with my aggression. I wanted out, but I was told that if I didn't do as I was asked, I'd be ratted out, all blame placed on me, and my career and life would be ended in one fatal swoop. Listen, I love you, Carissa, I love Sean..."

"Love ain't nothing but a word, coming from your lips. The world will see what you've done, what you all did. Unfortunately, Samara had to die, and the truth was hidden for nearly five years."

"She should have listened," he mumbles through his tears.

"Excuse me? She should have what?" I ask, making sure I've heard him correctly.

"She should have listened..."

Yep, I heard him correctly.

"Oh, so was she one of the young men and women *you* decided to place judgment on? One of the ones you just told me that didn't *deserve* help?"

No answer, he just stares.

"If you have something to say, say it! The cat's out of the bag now, and it won't be long before you and the rest of your dirty ass friends at that rinky-dink ass police station are taken down. They're on to each one of you. You're all going down."

"You can't blame this on me! You can't!"

"I can, and I will! The Lord says don't place judgement, and I'll have to ask for forgiveness later, but I'm placing judgment on you right now for what you did. Only God knows how many men and women you've killed or had a hand in killing and covering up. You know, I read through the statements that all of you gave. You all pulled together and gave such strong stories and alibis that no one ever questioned why she was beaten so badly, they only assumed it was from the arrest. For years I've wanted revenge, and the Lord places us into one another's paths and gets the revenge for me. How sweet is this!" I throw my hands up to the heavens.

He steps to me, looking me dead in the eye, and growls, "If she hadn't been actin' like a nigga, she wouldn't be dead."

Like a moment frozen in time, my body stops, completely frozen, processing the words Reese just allowed to slip from his tongue. And like a flashback in a movie, conversations that Reese and I had come back to me as if they just happened. The incident from the grocery store where he first met Sean and the incident in the restaurant, he was showing me signs then, but I didn't see them. Let me not forget all the dreams of snakes and other slippery serpents that have been recurring since I first met Reese. The Lord was showing me signs, but I foolishly ignored them all because I was caught up in being in love. I was in love with the idea of finding love for the second time in my lifetime. I was so caught up with what *could* be that I overlooked what actually was. I invited the devil into my life, my home, my heart, my body.

In a rage, I pick up a vase from my coffee table and hit Reese with it. He staggers but doesn't fall.

"You crazy bitch! I will make you pay!"

"Yeah, come on! This is the real you! I see you now, you damn devil!! You 'ol Uncle Tom ass negro! I see you!"

"Get out!" Sean steps in, hollering at the top of his lungs.

"Sean..." Reese states, but is interrupted by Sean, saying,

"Don't...just don't. If my Mom wants you out, then you leave...or I'll flush you out."

"Flush me out? All of my police talk rubbing off on you?"

"Nothing you've done will ever rub off on me. Ever!" Sean pulls out a gun.

"Sean! Where did you get that?" I say calmly as possible not to freak him out.

"You think you a man now, Sean? Huh?" Reese asks, walking toward the front door.

"More of a man than you will ever be. I'll make sure of that..." Sean grits, stepping toward Reese, gun pointed at him.

Sean fires the gun at Reese's feet, blowing a hole in my living room floor. My heart is in my throat, beating a thousand miles a minute. Internally I'm shouting, praying, for Sean not to fire again. The last thing I'd want him to do is to shoot Reese and end up in the system. Nothing would be more diffi-cult for me right now than losing another child over a man who practically killed my daughter. Losing another child to Reese, I would have to kill him myself, and anyone else who stands in my path.

"I won't ask again. We want you out, don't ever come back. You came into our lives, tricked us into loving you, only to find out you've betrayed us."

"I didn't betray you, Sean, please believe that. You just don't understand the caliber of events, things that I've had to deal with during the last few years of my life."

"I DON'T CARE WHAT YOU ENDURED! You don't just kill people for sport! You killed my sister, an innocent person, and we'll never be able to get her back. When she died, my mother died with her. Until you came along, Mom was empty, lost, completely lifeless. You helped bring her back, and now you've snatched it away. There's nothing about you that I could ever look up to."

Unaware of what might occur next, I whisper to Sean, asking for the gun but he ignores me. I know he doesn't want to do this, I can tell from the way his hands are trembling. As I talk him down more, he relaxes his arms, removing his hand from the trigger. I grab the gun, taking Sean into my embrace.

"Where did you get that?" I ask frantically as Reese makes his escape.

"In Dad's things..." Sean weeps, still a bit shaky, but we're interrupted by the sound of sirens.

Before I can react, police and ambulances are on my front lawn. I release Sean and run outside to see what the commotion is.

"You have the right to remain silent, anything you say can and will be used against you in the court of law..." an officer reads Reese his Miranda rights.

The look on his face as they read him his rights is golden. All that evilness, that wrongdoing, has finally caught up to him. I don't care how much he's changed, he will never surmount those he's had a hand in killing or has put behind bars out of spite, bitterness, or pure evilness.

"Mrs. C?" a familiar voice calls out for me.

I turn, it's Tyson.

"Tyson! Hi! Thank God you're here. What's all this?"

"Tonight's the night we decided to make our move. We're getting all these bastards who were involved with Samara's death, as well as the deaths of others. We got them, Mrs. C. We got them!"

"But, wait, how did you know where he'd be? How'd you know to find him here?"

Pointing to my house, Tyson says, "Ask him."

I look back at my home. I see Sean standing in the doorway with the ultimate look of satisfaction on his face. It was him, he called the police on Reese.

"Turns out the day you discovered Reese's name on that list, so did he. He only recently called me and told me about Reese, wanting help getting him out of your lives for good. After Reese arrived at your house tonight, Sean called and confided in me, so I knew it was time to make my move. I called my team and here we are, taking down the man who could have saved Samara but pulled that noose tighter instead. Go to Sean, comfort him."

I take off running to the house, and Tyson yells to me, "Mrs. C, Sean's going to make one hell of a man one day!"

EPILOGUE

Tyson was right, Sean learned Reese's name was on the list the same night that I did. Tyson's partner revealed the list to Sean, not knowing we knew Reese. Thinking back on it, Sean held this secret in for a few months, not saying a word. But now I can recall him acting a bit different, more distant than he did previously with Reese. Reese questioned it, but I reassured him it was nothing. I'm still pissed at myself for allowing Reese into my life. I should have been smarter, I should have questioned more things, I should have done more research. Unfortunately, I can't dwell on that now.

———

"Sean, come on, we're going to be late."

"Mom, you'll want to see this!" Sean hollers out.

I find him fixated on the television watching the news.

"What's this?"

"Just listen..." he uses the remote to increase the volume.

"It was discovered today that a gentleman by the name of Elvin Parks was found hanging in the same jail and cell that the late Samara Bennett was found in. Folks, is this a coincidence, or is there something corrupt going on beneath the surface? More for you after the commercial break."

The news reporter stands just outside the jail Samara was in, reporting another African American, a male, was found dead, hung. It's not a coincidence. When will people wake up? When will our people wake up and finally seek retribution? When will they realize that we are being targeted? How many more of us must die before we are equal...before our lives matter?

"Come on, baby, let's go," I tell Sean, highly disturbed by the news report.

———

Today's a huge day, as I sit in a courtroom watching as my attorney goes toe to toe with the attorney who's representing each of the gentlemen who was involved in Samara's death. One by one, each man takes the stand, admitting the truth about what occurred in that grimy cell in the early morning hours of July 31, 2015. The stories they tell, though they are the truth, are quite gruesome and heartless. The young man that recorded it all had the most to say and based on his demeanor you can tell that he's still traumatized from the event. After Samara's death, he left the law enforcement profession and sought another.

The newly released footage from Samara's cell is playing for the jury and audience to see, as well as the video footage from the young officer. The jury and audience are appalled and immediately disgusted by the acts of men who took an oath to protect and serve.

After deliberation, the jury has made its decision.

"You may all be seated. The jury has decided regarding the brutal death of Ms. Samara Brielle Bennett. In the case of Officer Tommy Gibson, you are found guilty..." the judge states firmly. "In the case of Officer Gregory Luckett, you are found guilty..."

Someone in the crowd begins to clap but is quickly silenced.

"And in the case of Samara Bennett, inmate number 02071987, Officer Reese Thompson, you are found guilty of murder in the first degree..." the judge begins to speak and my heart shatters. As he reads off Reese's charges, I'm immediately reminded of our time together, the monster that I let into my life. The judge sentenced each man to the max, the death penalty. They will all get a lethal injection for their crimes.

As the judge dismisses, Reese looks back at me and hollers out, "Carissa, I'm so sorry that you had to see me this way. I love you...I love Sean!"

I look around the courtroom in shame, as up to this point no one knew of my relationship with Reese. If they didn't, they surely do now, and they will soon be asking questions. I can only imagine that it'll be like reliving Samara's passing again; the questions, the news reporters, the cameras.

With Sean in tow, I make my way to the front entrance of the courthouse. As Sean and I open the doors, we find a mob of people waiting, watching, with signs in hand.

"NO JUSTICE, NO PEACE"
"BLACK LIVES MATTER"
"YOU WON'T BE SILENCED"
"WE WON'T FORGET"

There are so many signs that I can't make sense of them all.

As Sean and I step out into the crowd, we're embraced by everyone, as if we're all one big family. I've gotta admit, this feels good.

————

1 Year Later

"Today, we embark on a new journey. A journey filled with new life and hope for our community. Today we come together as one to celebrate a life that was taken from us too soon. We cannot bring her back, but we can honor her time here on earth. She left her footprint, and it will be up to us, all of us, to ensure your vision lives on and positively affects not only this community but communities around the nation," the mayor speaks. "Without further wait, I want to introduce Samara Bennett Boulevard."

The street sign on the corner of what is now known as Samara Bennett Boulevard and Poplar Ave is unveiled for the public eye. It's a beautiful sight. I guess after discovering the true story behind Samara's death, the city council had a change of heart regarding the street name change.

"Hold on folks, we've got one more surprise. As you can see, the building right here behind us has been restored to its original state and beyond. I'll allow Mrs. Carissa Bennett to speak."

The crowd whistles and applauds as I step up.

"First, thank you all for being here today. Your presence means everything to me. You could have been elsewhere, but here you are. As you all know by now, we received a large settlement for Samara's death; $1.9 million to be exact. That is no longer a secret. That money has been solely dedicated to this building. This building is officially known as the Samara Bennett Foundation, devoted to aiding people in the neighborhood and other low-income families when it comes to dealing with legal matters. This is a project which Samara held near and dear to her heart and I plan to carry that out for her. For what she endured, that's the least I could do. That's the least all of us could do."

"Mrs. Bennett, you and Sean should do the honors," the Mayor states, handing over a large pair of scissors.

With Sean holding the top and me holding the bottom, we open and close the scissors in unison, cutting the yellow ribbon covering the pathway to the Samara Bennett Foundation building.

———

"Sean, wake up. We're here," I shake him, putting the car into park.

I grab my bag from the back and walk alongside Sean, Stephanie, Tyson, and a host of neighbors and friends to Samara and Sam's gravesite.

From my small bag, I pull out a medium-sized blanket, spreading it over the ground right before my feet. Sean and I crouch down sitting between either grave. We sit and watch while everyone pays their respects, even Tyson. He says he's only been here once since she passed. He hasn't been able to bear coming here to see her like this. I can't say that I blame him. She's my child and it's hard to see her this way. He lays a dozen golden Calla Lilies at the head of her grave. He always bought them for her, therefore they became her favorite.

I spend a few moments at Sam's grave, then over to Samara's.

"You know, I thought your grandmother was crazy when she suggested I name you Samara. I had a different name in mind for you, like Juliet or Savannah, or something. On the day I went into labor, your grandmother asked me one last time what your name was to be. I asked her why she was so adamant about naming you, Samara. She said the name had meaning. I don't believe I ever told you, maybe she did, but Samara is Hebrew, and it means guardian or protected by God. I know I couldn't protect you, but God has and will continue to use a host of people to do the work you started during your time here," I speak, eyes closed, hands planted on her stone.

After saying my goodbyes, I stand and we all gather hands, forming a circle around Sam and Samara's grave.

"Baby girl, you are no longer Inmate Number 02071987, you are Samara B. Bennett, protected by God. May you rest in eternal peace and love. We shall meet again soon."

MESSAGE FROM THE AUTHOR

We're not born with hatred in our hearts. Hate is taught. But unless we're strong enough to stand up for what we know is right, confront those we know are wrong, then we're no better than those who are spreading the hatred.
"Darkness cannot drive out darkness; only light can do that. Hate cannot drive out hate; only love can do that."

-MLK

MEET THE AUTHOR

Kierra Walker

Author Kierra Walker is an Arkansas native, her roots embedded in the southeast region of the state.

Walker has garnered much acclaim for her bestselling titles *Saving Grace* and *Inmate #02071987* and has successful published a number of other bestselling titles.

Kierra's eclectic, compassionate, and charismatic nature serves as the foundational layer to each storyline she pens.

Join Kierra Walker as She grants readers access to the innermost portions of her mind through heartfelt classics with captivating narratives, hints of drama, and comedic flair.

www.ingramcontent.com/pod-product-compliance
Lightning Source LLC
Chambersburg PA
CBHW072233290326
41934CB00008BA/1269